Contents

List of Figures and Tables   vii

Preface   ix

Acknowledgements   xiii

1. An overview of reading and its teaching   1
2. Changes in thinking about reading   16
3. A decade of reading research   31
4. Reading research in the UK   52
5. Towards a framework for rethinking and teaching reading   90
6. Teaching reading in the infant school   98
7. Teaching reading in the junior school   115
8. Conspectus   128

Appendix 1   List of books used in research   131
Appendix 2   Means, standard deviations of standard errors for Analysis technique 1   133
Appendix 3   Register indexical word lists   141
Appendix 4   Piggy-bank example   143

Appendix 5   Examples of categorization for
             Analysis technique 2   145

Appendix 6   Different types of genre styles   149

References   151

Index   157

List of Figures and Tables

Figures

1. Rank scale for the lexicogrammar of English (p.19)
2. The text-forming component of the semantic system (p.21)
3. An example of schema (p.35)
4. Examples of propositions (p.37)
5. The syntactic structures of the story (p.38)
6. Examples from Isolated, Tied and Context version booklets (p.62)
7. The Reading Development Continuum (p.76)
8. Summary of criteria for allocating reponses (p.77)
9. Excerpt from *A Stuart Family in the Civil War* (p.78)
10. Example of semantic field data (p.81)
11. Individual RDC Profiles (High performers) (p.84)
12. Individual RDC Profiles (Medium performers) (p.84)
13. Individual RDC Profiles (Low performers) (p.84)
14. RDC for poor reader (Fiction) 8 years old (p.85)
15. RDC for poor reader (Factual) 8 years old (p.85)
16. RDC for poor reader (Fiction) 9 years old (p.86)
17. RDC for poor reader (Factual) 9 years old (p.86)
18. RDC for poor reader (Fiction) 10 years old (p.87)
19. RDC for poor reader (Factual) 10 years old (p.87)

A1 Cohort A. Ravens Matrices (p.68)
A2 Cohort A. Standardized Reading Tests (p.68)
A3 Cohort A. Cohesion (Fiction) Tests (p.69)
A4 Cohort A. Cohesion (Factual) Tests (p.69)

B1 Cohort B. Ravens Matrices (p.70)
B2 Cohort B. Standardized Reading Tests (p.70)
B3 Cohort B. Cohesion (Fiction) Tests (p.71)
B4 Cohort B. Cohesion (Factual) Tests (p.71)

C1   Cohort C. Ravens Matrices (p.72)
C2   Cohort C. Standardized Reading Tests (p.72)
C3   Cohort C. Cohesion (Fiction) Tests (p.73)
C4   Cohort C. Cohesion (Factual) Tests (p.73)

H1   Histogram of Children's Reading Progress over 3 years (p.83)

Tables

4(1)   Consensus on the temporal conjunction 'then' (p.65)
4(2)   Consensus, number of different responses, proportion of exact responses for one item from two groups of 10 year olds (p.66)
4(3)   Consensus, number of different responses and proportion of exact responses for 3 substitute items for 3 age groups (p.67)

Preface

This book is addressed to teachers and others associated with children learning how to read in primary or elementary schools. As such it is also an update of a book published a few years ago. (Chapman 1983). Like that book it assumes that reading has a privileged place in the curriculum for it is not only the gateway to a fundamental part of our culture but has recently been shown to have profound effects on the mind's development (Miller 1972; Donaldson 1978), that is, capacity for disembedded or decontextualized thought. Although there are critics of this stance (Street 1984), it is, nonetheless, a most important phenomenon which we need to take seriously and we will be looking at it further in Chapter 3.

You might be forgiven for thinking, 'What, another book about reading?' and wonder why you should be bothered to read it. However, apart from providing an update on thinking about reading, there are serious grounds for drawing your attention to some research that shows that all is still not well in schools as far as the teaching of reading is concerned.

If we look first at the products of our schools, we find in a recent study by Mary Hamilton that 10 per cent of 23 year olds, who were interviewed as part of the National Child Development Study in 1981, reported problems with reading, writing and spelling since leaving school. 'They most frequently mentioned employment contexts as causing difficulties or presenting obstacles' (ALBSU 1987). These findings tie in with employers' complaints about the literacy weakneeses of potential employees. And while the latter could be construed as a political point, because employers appear to have been complaining since the 1920s as recorded by the Newbold Committee (HMSO 1921), we cannot gainsay the feelings of inadequacy expressed by the young people themselves, It could, of course, be said that the employers may have been correct for more than half a century!

There is also evidence, for example, of what has been termed 'a retreat from print' (Lunzer and Gardner 1979) in some of our secondary schools. And this evidence, together with that produced in an Open University survey which extends and confirms these findings, will be shown in Chapter 3 and 4. This is despite what might be gathered from the surveys of the Assessment and Performance Unit where there is little reported on the size, depth and seriousness of the problem. And we understand that other countries, who share English with us as their mother tongue, have similar problems. In a survey of literacy and reading performance in the United States from 1880 to the present, Stedman and Kaestle (1987) point out that, although the 'reading achievement for a given age level has been stable throughout most of the twentieth century', things are not rosy on the literacy front. They state:

> Results of the functional literacy tests suggest that a substantial portion of the population, from 20 to 30 per cent, have difficulty coping with common reading tasks and materials. The job literacy measures, for all their limitations, have detected substantial mismatches between many workers' literacy skills and the reading demands of their jobs. Even if schools are doing about as well as they have in the past, they have never done well in educating minorities and the poor or in teaching high-order skills.
>
> (Stedman and Kaestle 1987:42)

In whatever way this present situation might be explained, the facts suggest strongly that there is an urgent need for teachers to take stock and rethink their prevailing conceptualization of reading and the organization of its teaching.

Unfortunately there is insufficient in-service training to update teachers with advances in thinking and one provider, the Open University whose courses in language and reading have been taken by thousands of teachers, no longer has the resources to carry on with this line of teaching. We have to rely therefore on books such as those in this series to keep teachers up to date.

In addition to these factors we are living in what has been called an age of information. The extent of the worldwide flow of information and who controls it are further weighty questions of international proportions. The controlling agent is the modern computer and it is clear that if, as a nation, we are to face the demands of a highly technical age, then children's familiarity with computers is a prime necessity. Apart from this there are good reasons for using the computer in schools for the enhancement of many literacy activities as well as the management of pupil progress.

It is clear that schools are faced with new challenges and we suggest that for those teachers who wish to meet them, these challenges will involve some or all of the following:

- keeping up to date in both theory and practice by becoming more aware of new knowledge and new attitudes to research.
- meeting the developmental needs of children of all ages so as to prepare them adequately for the present and future demands of their education.
- realizing the extent of language and language-related knowledge that has been taken for granted in the classroom or remains implicit when helping children learn to read.
- fostering a continuing desire in children to become readers in the full sense of that term.
- maintaining an interest in computer developments in education and their implications for use in the classroom.

It is not possible in one short volume, however, to deal adequately with all these factors, so some, which are more applicable to later schooling, will be addressed further in other volumes in this series. They will include more of the findings of the OU cohesion research project as they apply to children's reading in the secondary school.

The first four chapters of this book begin an analysis of literacy problems and provide a summary of some of the research into reading that has taken place recently. As a consequence of this you are invited in Chapter 5 to rethink your ideas about reading and how children learn to read. It is hoped that by facing these challenges you will gain a greater understanding of the reading requirements of your pupils. The later chapters outline proposals for reading and the organization of its teaching in classrooms. Chapters 6 and 7 are structured to suggest answers to five classroom-based questions. These are:

1. What aspects of reading should be encouraged within any one particular age group and how can recent research on reading development help us to achieve this?
2. What teaching strategies will meet those needs?
3. What teaching methods are applicable in this situation?
4. How might the teaching so designed be evaluated?
5. How might the children's reading progress be monitored?

These elements may assist you to teach all the children for whom you are responsible to read more enjoyably and effectively.

In Chapter 8 the aims of the book are reviewed by way of a conspectus.

Acknowledgements

As with most books, many colleagues and friends contribute much to the development of the ideas that are portrayed; and this book is no exception. In this case a group of teachers, lecturers and students met regularly to discuss with me, and each other, the teaching implications of the concepts of cohesion and register. I owe a debt of gratitude to this group for their consistent support and contributions, particularly to one of the systems of analysis that was devised to analyse the data from the reading survey. Although others joined us from time to time, regular members of the group were Elizabeth Wishart, Sylvia Winchester, Peter Spode, Bobbie Neate and Eleanor Anderson. Recently they have been joined by Alison Littlefair who is making a study of genre and register.

In addition, Professor Jonathan Anderson of the Flinders University of South Australia has made a significant contribution. He wrote the GAP computer program for the quantitative analysis of the data and a number of microcomputer programs related to the research for use in schools.

The staff of the Academic Computer Service at the Open University, particularly Richard Austin, must also be acknowledged for their considerable help with the handling of large amounts of data.

Mention must be made of Professor Eunice Schmidt of Seattle Pacific University for she and her students have given the research an international dimension.

Finally, I must thank my family for their forbearance while I pursued this work over many years.

Dr L. John Chapman,
Romsley, Worcestershire,
June 1987.

CHAPTER 1

An overview of reading and its teaching

Many adults learned to read successfully and have found reading a pleasure since their earliest days. It is likely that you are among them. Many of these natural readers neither remember being taught how to read nor did they experience problems with their reading. They appear to have come to terms with the process in much the same way as they learned to speak, that is, naturally. Of these readers it might be said that they took to reading like ducks take to water. Indeed it has been observed recently that there is nothing special or unique about reading; Smith (1978) tells us that no part of the brain deals exclusively with reading. We use many of the same brain functions for reading as we do for speaking and listening. This may be so as far as general intellectual processes are concerned but, as we noted in the Preface, we are still faced with a serious situation where many of the younger generation leave school unable to function adequately as readers in the complex society in which they are to operate. It follows also that they will not become readers in the full sense of that term and enjoy reading for pleasure. At first sight then there appears to be a paradox: some learn to read effortlessly, quickly mastering its complexities, while others achieve but a smattering of reading after many years of near failure. And here it must be stressed that it is not just those who need specialist attention in what were once termed remedial groups that are being referred to but those who are termed average and below in the school situation.

In order to find answers to these dilemmas we turn first to the study of reading to learn a little of the current thinking and what it can offer by way of explanation of the complicated process of reading.

The study of reading

The study of reading and learning to read has a long and interesting history to which many disciplines, philosophy, psychology, sociology, linguistics, anthropology and the information theorists, have contributed. Psychology was early in the field at the beginning of the century and has been prominent since, particularly during the last two decades. Much of this work involves sensory perception, memory, comprehension, psychometrics and latterly information processing, especially as seen by cognitive psychologists. Indeed many psychologists still maintain Huey's now classic statement to be as relevant today as it was at the beginning of the century:

> And so to completely analyse what we do when we read would almost be the acme of a psychologist's achievements, for it would be to describe many of the most intricate workings of the human mind, as well as to unravel the tangled story of the most remarkable specific performance that civilisation has learned in all its history.
>
> (Huey 1908:6)

Reading and the development of thinking

Huey's statement is of considerable interest because recently the study of reading has begun to show how very important reading is for the mind's development. Miller (1972) makes the point that writing did not begin as a means for encoding speech as some might think. 'Talking and writing', he states, 'seem to have evolved separately and grown together later.' He highlights the effects that the 'wide adoption of writing and reading' had on Greek culture and selects the rejection of myth and its replacement by history, and the invention of logic as the most important intellectual activities that become possible as a result of writing. He attributes these basic changes to the fact that 'their alphabetic writing objectified language, the product of thought, and give it a permanence that the spoken word lacked.' The same is true of memory in that writing objectified personal memory.

For logic however, he finds a more subjective explanation, drawing attention to the written proposition being a 'tangible representation of an act of thought'. This recording of thought, he proposes, makes it possible 'to react to one's own thoughts.' He believes this to be the more significant of the two in that it directly affected the way the mind works.

Margaret Donaldson reaches much the same conclusion as a result of her studies. She has written about the effect of reading on the developing mind. In this, she believes that the decontextual nature of texts has far-reaching effects. The written word is unlike speech or conversation which takes place in the 'here and now' where the setting is obvious to both parties. In speech also some of the meaning is conveyed by intonation, as in a question where the sounds of the words follow a rising tone. A certain amount is conveyed by gesture and in other non-verbal ways. None of these are present, however, to help the reader of a written text. But more important for the point being made here is the context of the situation, in which the conversation is taking place, as this can be considered to be an actual part of the meaning being transmitted. Items in a room, for example, can be referred to by a gesture without words actually being used to name and describe them. These factors, together with the ephemeral nature of speech, which unless recorded is soon forgotten, all add up to the fact that speech leaves little choice of meaning. In written language, however, an actual physical context is not available and the author has to replace it by providing the reader with a context. In this respect, the author expects readers to infer the meaning not only from the clues given directly in the text but from their own background knowledge of similar situations with which they are familiar. This background knowledge, or prior knowledge as it is sometimes called, is said to be stored in memory in *schemata* and there is a body of psychological research, some of which we review in Chapter 3, dealing with it. Although writing only provides a little of the richness of the context of speech, nonetheless it has one very important characteristic; it makes speech visible and permanent. This permanency, as Miller suggests, is most important for it enables the developing mind to consider different possibilities as to what the text means. Donaldson comments about this:

> Thus it turns out that those very features of the written word which encourage awareness of language may also encourage awareness of ones's own thinking and be relevent to the development of intellectual control, with incalculable consequences for the development of the kinds of thinking which are characteristic of logic, mathematics and the sciences.
>
> (Donaldson 1978:95).

This close relationship between reading, writing and thinking is crucial in education, and we will be returning to it in Chapter 3, where we also look at some of the criticisms of these claims. Next we see how thinking about the reading process itself has progressed in the last decade.

The reading process

If you ask any adult how they or their children learned to read, one of the most frequent answers given will refer to learning the alphabet, the ABC, and the sounds associated with the letters. It would appear that learning how to read print is conceived of as learning to break a code. This being so, it would follow that learning to decipher the code would give access to the sounds of language and then, presumably by using the same mental processes that are used in understanding speech, the reader would arrive at the meaning encoded in the text.

In explaining what it is about reading that is being learned the analogy of a code is useful as language is a symbolic system, a system of signs. However, the study of reading reveals that the code is more complex than it first appears.

The nature of the code

One of the characteristics noted about skilled readers is that it is not necessary for them to distinguish every letter during reading or indeed the detail of every word. There are more features to letters, their individual shapes, than is absolutely necessary for their instant recognition. We call this property *redundancy,* a term we will use again when considering other language topics. It has been proposed by Goodman that readers only sample as much of the print as is necessary to confirm their predictions of the passage's meaning. He puts it thus:

> Reading at its proficient best is a smooth, rapid, guessing game in which the reader samples from available language cues, using the least amount of available information to achieve this essential task of reconstructing and comprehending the writer's meaning. It can be regarded as a systematic reduction of uncertainty as the reader starts with the graphic input and ends with meaning.
>
> (Goodman 1970:27)

For the moment it is sufficient to note that to select only parts of the letters (the most significant being the top parts), or indeed to select words for attention and ignore the rest, will involve some cognitive capacity which controls what sensory stimuli we attend to as we read.

Another feature of the code is that a direct one to one correspondence of letters and sounds assumed by many just does not exist in the English writing system. For example, sometimes we use the same two letters, 'oo' and 'ee', to represent one sound, or different letters are grouped, as in 'ch' and 'ng', when separately they have other sounds. One of the major problems is that there are so many rules for children to learn and to guide them as to how the system works. Indeed, Berdiansky *et al* (1969) found when they studied 6,000 words from books used by six to nine year olds some degree of regularity in 211 different spellings whereas 661 words, more than one in 10, had to be classified as 'exceptions' and 166 rules had to be devised to cover the remaining 5,431 words. Sixty of these rules concerned the pronunciation of consonants which are usually considered to be 'regular'. The problem is illustrated tellingly by the following poem:

> Hints on pronunciation for foreigners
>
> I take it you already know
> Of tough and bough and cough and dough?
> Others may stumble but not you,
> On hiccough, thorough, laugh and through.
> Well done! And now you wish, perhaps,
> To learn of less familiar traps?
> Beware of heard, a dreadful word
> That looks like beard and sounds like bird,
> And dead: it's said like bed, not bead—
> For goodness sake don't call it 'deed'!
> Watch out for meat and great and threat
> (That rhyme with suite and straight and debt).
> A moth is not a moth in mother
> Nor both in bother, broth in brother,
> And here is not a match for there
> Nor dear and fear for bear and pear,
> Just look them up—and goose and choose,

And cork and work and card and ward,
And font and front and word and sword,
And do and go and thwart and cart–
Come, come, I've hardly made a start!
A dreadful language? Man alive.
I'd mastered it when I was five.
       T.S.W (only initials known)
   From a letter published in the Sunday Times on 3rd January 1965 (cited in Mackay, Thompson and Schaub, 1968)

   In addition, although there are meaning relationships between some words that influence their spelling, their pronunciation alters when they are extended, for instance 'nation' becomes 'national' and 'sign' becomes 'signal'.
   But the nature of the code and the ramifications of the alphabetic system, complicated as they are, are only a part of the process that has to be mastered. In order to help our understanding of such an intricate system it is customary to try to model it. Such models are, of course, abstractions from what happens in practice but they do have a practical use, that is, to enable us to make predictions about such complex processes as reading.

Top-down, bottom-up and interactive models of reading

The goal of reading is to understand what has been written, so learning to read involves learning how to make meaning from print. Some models of reading assume that the process begins, as we have seen with the code, with the written or printed letters on a page, moving progressively through letters and words to larger linguistic units like sentences and paragraphs until the meaning of the complete text is reached. Such models have been termed bottom-up models and have been contrasted by those which are supposed to operate in a top-down fashion. In this, it is proposed that the process begins first in the mind of the reader and that a series of hypotheses are made as to the meaning residing in the print to be read. These hypotheses are then either confirmed or rejected as the reader proceeds.

Bottom-up models

An early version of the bottom-up type was proposed by Phillip Gough at a conference held in 1971 entitled 'Language by Ear and Eye' (Kavanagh and Mattingly 1972). In his paper, Gough looked at 'one second of reading' and attempted to show what happens (at lightning speed of course) from the moment when the reader's eye fixates on the first letter of the first word of the first sentence to the moment a second later when the reader speaks the word. The time span of one second is divided up into milliseconds and what is thought to happen within intervals of approximately 100 milliseconds is accounted for by the model.

There are two main features of Gough's model that are of interest. Firstly, the model assumes that meaning is arrived at by a process that moves in a step by step fashion from the smallest feature of the letters on the page to the comprehension of a sentence, memory being used for processing and storage of the detailed information received. Secondly, the route taken to construct meaning at word level is via the sound system which has been acquired during learning to speak.

Gough has (Gough 1985) admitted that his model is wrong, but he also points out that other models when 'interactive or transactional enough' are empty. He does state, however,

> The hallmark of the skilled reader is the ability to recognize, accurately, easily, and swiftly, isolated words (and, even more so, pseudo words). We have argued elsewhere....that this skill can only be attributed to the ability to decode, for while highly predictive context can and does facilitate word recognition, proving a strictly 'bottom-up' model like mine wrong, most words are not predictable and so can only be read bottom up. A successful model of reading must account for this ability. My model may have failed, but I still believe it pointed in the right direction.
>
> (Gough 1985:688)

Top-down models

The model that is often quoted as being an example of top-down processing is provided by Goodman (1970). One of the main differences between this and Gough's psychological model is its psycholinguistic nature. Goodman believes that reading is not exclusively a psychological process or a language process but a combination of both. He emphasizes the fundamental importance of its langue base, stating that 'To understand how reading works one must understand how language works'. He points out that:

> Written language is a display of letters. Letters are composed of straight and curved line segments, and form letter groupings which are separated by white space. But meaning can be derived from written language only when underlying clauses and their interrelationships have been inferred. Thus, the most significant unit in reading is not the letter, word or sentence, but the clause.
>
> (Goodman 1970:26)

Three basic kinds of linguistic information are used in the model, the symbol sytem (sound or graphic), language structure or syntax and the semantic or meaning system. The model envisages these systems operating in cyclic fashion with a visual input. It suggests that readers move more or less sequentially through these cycles with the focus on meaning. Goodman stresses, 'the readers' focus, if they are to be productive, is on meaning. The cycles are telescoped by the readers if they can get meaning. That is, proficient readers can go directly to the meaning of the passage being read, only sampling the print for confirmation of the hypotheses they have made about the meaning intended by the author. In no way is the process conceived of as moving sequentially along the lines of print as in Gough's model.

There are then three basic characteristics of the top-down model. These are, firstly, the influence of the readers meaning predictions and their control during perception; secondly, the most significant language unit, psychologically speaking, is not the *letter* or *word* (in Goodman's psycholinguistic model), but the clause; and thirdly, there is a hypothesis testing procedure which checks predictions emanating from the 'top', using as many of the cueing systems as necessary to confirm the meaning hypotheses.

An interactive model

Attempts have been made to combine the strengths of these two models, and we should note in passing that there are no exclusively top-down or bottom-up positions. To illustrate a further development we choose Rumelhart's (1977) interactive model. Rumelhart suggest that reading is clearly both a perceptual and a cognitive process and he specifies how the interaction between the two is psychologically plausible. Drawing on the work of computer scientists, he devised a model of reading using two computer programs. Rumelhart calls the communications centre of his model the 'message centre' and this is where the input from the senses is received.

The model consists largely of a series of 'knowledge sources', each of which is independent and contains specialized knowledge of the reading process. Each knowledge source constantly scans the message centre for hypotheses relevant to that particular source, evaluates any that are found and confirms or discards them.

There are similarities to both the other models mentioned above. Interestingly, in spite of the complexity of an interactive system, the model can focus on either top-down or bottom-up elements.

The importance of modelling, and the accounts we have given are only brief sketches, are the implications that arise from them for teaching. The top-down model leads to giving a 'meaning' emphasis in learning in read whereas the bottom-up lends itself to a 'code' emphasis. We will be meeting this again later in the chapters on teaching.

Reading as language development

Most attempts at modelling the reading process come from psychologists and psycholinguists. Another major influence, however, has come from a different discipline, that of linguistics or language study. The extent of the growth and influence of linguistics has been dramatic during the period under review.

It has often been observed, and it is every parent's experience, that most children acquire spoken language effortlessly from their immediate kinsfolk. Yet this process is not completely inborn. It could happen, for example, that a child born of English parents, then orphaned and reared from babyhood in

China in a Mandarin speaking family will pick up Mandarin rather than English as his or her first language. This would seem self-evident but the very ubiquity and speed of early language learning conceals some very subtle processes which we are only just beginning to understand. What has not been appreciated are the considerable ramifications of this process, because not only will that orphan become a fluent speaker of Mandarin but will acquire much of Chinese culture simultaneously with its language. And more important still, as children mature, they will gain, albeit largely without conscious awareness, an understanding of the inter-relationships between their culture and its language. This will enable them to produce the type of language variety required by the varying situations in which they find themselves. In most cases they will not realize this, as much linguistic or language awareness is implicit and only becomes explicit when the child is older (and only then sometimes when attention is drawn to features of language).

Linguistic awareness

It would seem that children do not have the ability to look at language itself as distinct from being users of it until about the age of seven. Margaret Donaldson points this out:

> The child's awareness to what he talks about–the things out there to which the language refers–normally takes precedence over his awareness of what he talks with–the words he uses. And he becomes aware of what he talks with–the actual words–before he is at all aware of the rules which control the production of them. (Indeed a thoughtful adult has a very limited awareness of such processes in his own mind.)
>
> (Donaldson 1978: 87–88)

The dawn of awareness of the sounds of language have been documented by Weir (1962) who recorded the experimentation of her child with the sounds of language while still in the crib. But this is before language has developed sufficiently for the child to be able to be aware of it in the sense we have in mind. We know when this time arrives for it is when parents and teachers are bombarded with jokes and riddles that rely on words being used out of context or with more than one meaning. And this is the time for teachers to begin to reveal with discovery type activities how language works (such teaching being distinct from children's use of language, but taught alongside it). We hasten to add here, as we will be developing this procedure for teaching purposes in later chapters, that this is not a call for the re-introduction of traditional grammar lessons but the beginning of an attempt to make the study of language a more exciting part of the curriculumn. It should be said that language is as interesting an academic subject as many others we teach. It has as much, or even greater importance and relevance than many others that crowd the curriculum.

Only recently have we begun to realize the enormous implications that arise from these heretofore hidden language awareness factors and the great possibilities that they offer the teacher who knows about them. The reappraisal of reading as a language process brings new understandings which have direct relevance to classroom teaching situations, which we will show in later chapters. A large part of the thinking behind this book, its *raison d'être* if you like, rests upon a belief in the important practical implications that 'language awareness' has for the teaching of reading. By raising the level of teachers' awareness of reading as a language process, it is hoped that we can begin to help every child's reading development.

First language

In this country, although we are becoming a multilingual society the first langauge of the majority of children is still English. But note that it will be that variety of English spoken by the parents and often influenced by the geographical region in which they live. In the British Isles, as in other English-speaking countries, there are many regional dialects and these will become part of some children's real-life communication experience. Children in Yorkshire will speak not only with a Yorkshire accent, but understand local dialect, or vocabulary terms that children in other parts of the country will not readily comprehend. However, one variety of English has become the standard and it became thus because it is the variety spoken by those in power. Because of this it has inevitably become very influential. It has also been favoured by the educated and has much in common with written langage–the language of books. However, for some, Standard English and the regionless-accent (or Received Pronunciation (RP) as it is sometimes called) associated with it, remains almost another language. This does not imply that there are not many families in Yorkshire or in any other region that are not Standard English speakers, but that there are many that are proficient only in a non-standard version of English.

The main difference between Standard English and non-standard varieties lies in their grammars. Perera stresses this in the following way:

> We have already seen that Standard English can be spoken with either a regional or regionless pronunciation; so long as speech is comprehensible to the listeners, there is no reason why schools should attempt to alter their pupils' accents. What does matter, though, is whether the children's grammar is that of Standard English or one of the regional varieties.
>
> (Perera 1987)

It is for social reasons, however, that teachers are conceerned about the use of non-standard English. They are aware that their pupils will need to become Standard English users if they are to succeed in today's society. Quoting again from Perera, who sums up this position clearly:

blem, of course, is what I have called *different* grammar is to some extent gmatized; there is no denying that people who cannot speak or write rammar when the situation requires it can be at a considerable social ge.

(Perera 1987)

And this can extend, as we have seen from Hamilton's research mentioned in the Preface, to young people's job prospects.

Language in the home

It is a commonplace to observe that the language used in the home is a variety that the child is comfortable with, children are literally 'at home' using it. It contains many instances of everyday terms like pet names and family sayings that the child has contributed and has understood, therefore, since infancy. Most importantly perhaps, it is the vehicle that has been used to relay wants, to communicate with other members of the family, and, as we will see below, for a number of other functions, which add up to making meaning in and of the world. And yet, for the reasons given above, because of the great variety of homes and the difference of the home variety from the Standard, problems arise when the child moves from the home to the wider world outside. This often comes into prominence when the child begins formal schooling. This is not, as we have seen, because the language of the home is not expressive – meanings are conveyed very readily indeed – but that the child may not be able to comprehend the teacher fully in the new social situation of the school. Here the variety of language could be called educational and is nearer the Standard and, significantly in this context, nearer to the language of books.

Some parents, however, because of their backgrounds, prepare their children for this transfer to the world outside and to the school, not by any direct teaching, but by conveying the value they put on education as part of their lifestyle. They apply, in a natural fashion, their own cultural values daily to features that are recognized, however informally, as educational. Their children, before formal schooling, have already become comfortable with Standard English – it is after all the language of their home – and have acquired the values that will be highlighted by the school. Many will have attended playschools and toddlers' groups where they have become attuned to some of the features of Standard English. These factors apply particularly to literacy,which remains convincingly the hallmark of educated people.

You will begin to understand perhaps why, because of the level of literacy and values transmitted to them in interaction with their parents, some children slip into the school environment easily and painlessly. In many cases these children come into school already reading and writing and respecting what the teacher values, because these are the same values held by their parents and those they have known since their earliest years. These children have, to use the title of an American early literacy programme, a 'Headstart'.

Others, from a teacher's viewpoint, are not so fortunate. Their parents' values are different and their concerns are not academic as those of the schools are. This is not to say that they hold values any the less worthy. It is just that their immediate society has other values and standards. As we have already observed, the unfortuante part of this dilemma is that, for most, to get ahead in our present social situation involves complying with the Standard and achieving the ability to read and write for many different purposes.

There are yet others in our communities whose first language is not English and they have to learn a second language, the language of the dominant culture. Not only do they have to contend with this, but the local variety may also present them with additional problems as they try to learn Standard English. They have multi-lingual problems.

Having been introduced to the importance of language-cultural relationships you will not be surprised to find that children in these situations also find learning in school problematical, because language is the basis for much of school learning. It has been proposed that this problem could be largely overcome by teaching children, whose first language is other than English, in their own mother tongue. If we considered that the concepts to be engendered in the school are closely bound up with the language we use to teach them, then to have mother tongue teaching while the second language is being learned seems, at first sight, to be helpful. However, these proposals have become controversial and we leave them to another volume where we consider teaching in multicultural settings.

Nonetheless, in all these instances there is often a motivational force that comes from a set of values in the home that prizes education. Such a force will drive some children to overcome all the obstacles.

Emergent literacy

Recently researchers have begun to study afresh some of the factors involved in successful literacy development. The details of their findings when assembled provide a radically different picture of the way in which children acquire literacy than that to which some may have become accustomed. Two American investigators, Teale and Sulzby, have done much to document this change in understanding and we go on to relate some of their conclusions in this overview chapter.

First, there has been a major change in thinking regarding the notion that children are not ready to benefit from instruction in reading and writing until they go to school and have reached a certain level of mental maturity, often put at about six years. It has been held that to attempt to teach these skills prior to this stage in the child's development would be a waste of time, even detrimental. The concern for 'reading readiness', as it was known, was almost universal, influencing teachers and publishers alike. This was manifest in the curriculum in the infant school and in the materials produced by publishers for those schools.

Alongside this phenomenon was the belief that reading was an amalgam of sub-skills, and that each needed to be fully functioning before children could even begin to read their first books. There were many boxes of apparatus aimed at increasing children's ability in a variety of perceptual tasks. These usually consisted of games and puzzles attempting to train children to recognize the distinctive features of letter-like shapes by orientation and matching tasks. Reading was often delayed until these skills had been practised sufficiently and the age of so-called readiness was thought to have been reached.

In sharp contrast literacy is now thought of as emerging from the earliest years, long before the formal literacy instruction in school begins. This comes about because it has been observed that many children are involved informally in reading and writing activities in most homes very early in their young lives. These activities have just not been recognized for what they are. It is suggested that the beginnings of literacy have been misconceived and that the search and practice of skills, thought to be associated with reading and writing, was misguided.

Secondly, there is now a belief that children develop as reader/writers concurrently and that one of these skills does not precede the other. That is, reading does not precede writing or vice versa. Further, the different modes of language, speaking, listening, reading and writing, develop together, wholistically. These aspects of language are integrated during literacy development and not developed separately, in sequence.

The third point made by Teale and Sulzby is that literacy develops in real-life settings when children are engaged in activities that are purposeful. The need *to use* these aspects of literacy in their everyday life experiences is the driving force behind their development.

Fourthly, cognitive aspects relevent to literacy are developing during the years from birth to six years of age by which time most children are at school.

Children, it is suggested, explore print on their own and are influenced by adults in their immediate family or social grouping actively using literacy. The effect of such modelling has been discovered to be a significant environmental factor.

Finally, although there appear to be stages in literacy development that children pass through, they can do so in a number of ways and at different ages. As a consequence the preparation of programmes needs to take this into account.

These factors, you will surely agree, have far-reaching implications for the methods and strategies used in schools as well as the experiences gained in the children's homes'. We will be examining some of these implications in the chapters that follow and in doing so we will be adopting some of the concepts and terminology ('emergent literacy' for example) that we have introduced during this overview.

Home–school relationships

Much has been made in recent years of the benefits of close home–school relationships. No longer are doors closed to parents, on the contrary in many schools they are welcomed to take part in the life of the school and in some cases even to enter and help the teacher with the activities in the classroom. The ethos in many schools has changed remarkably in this respect during the last few years and investigations of some of these changes have produced most interesting research findings. This has been especially so in those cases concerned with direct parent–teacher cooperation where children's reading has been enhanced by the parent regularly hearing the child read, or reading with the child, at home (Tizard *et al.* 1982). This again underlines the strength of the home influence that we have noted earlier and is a force that teachers do well to harness. This research has been widely disseminated and many such programmes are in operation. However, they are not always successful and a word of caution is necessary for it is important not to be too caught up by the fervour surrounding some programmes. Rather you should sort out the best methods, particularly those programmes that have been evaluated (see Topping (1986) and Pumfrey (1986)). One method that we will be recommending is the original version of 'paired reading'. But there have been changes of another quite different type in some homes and we turn next to the implications of these.

The age of information and the microcomputer

It was claimed at a conference held in Scotland in 1984 that there were (at that time) more home computers per head of population in the UK than in any other country in the world. Apart from this statistic being quite surprising, it raises two important points. One concerns the way in which increasing technological sophistication has impinged on us all and the other the extent to which many children will have become accustomed to the language of computing in their homes. These children will be used to microcomputers, having none of the hang-ups that some adults tend to have with the new technologies. However, what we need to be aware of as educationalists are two other, less obvious, but more far-reaching, factors.

Two historical examples may serve to illustrate this point. These are taken from a number of 'micro tales' related by Anderson (1987) at the World Reading Conference in London. The first concerns the Incas and the way in which they communicated and stored the information that they used to control their empire which was, at its height, truly remarkable. All the information needed to administer it (the people had not discovered reading and writing) was stored on quipus, which were knotted coloured cords. The holder of these would be responsible for about 10 families, recording marriages, additions to the family, harvest yields and other items of importance. Runners carried the cords holding this information to the Inca who ruled the Empire. The control of information was achieved by having central store houses where the details of the country were kept for administrative purposes. It has been pointed out that their empire had been built up by access to and control of this information. It also contributed to their downfall, because the Spaniards, realizing its importance, destroyed the information stores. This crippled the means of communication and enabled a small number of Spaniards, in 1532, to effect a speedy conquest of that vast and rich empire.

Associated with the control of information is the speed at which information can now be transmitted and received by satellite across the world. The second example, which serves to illustrate this, is nearer in both time and space. An account of the Battle of Waterloo relates that news of Wellington's victory was relayed to London in a novel, but for those days speedy, fashion. The story has it that the Rothschilds, who had already invested heavily in the British armed forces during the conflict, increased their wealth considerably by having news of the defeat of Napoleon brought by carrier pigeon ahead of other financiers. Thus informed, the Rothschild family were able, by a few swift moves on the Stock Exchange, to increase their fortune considerably.

The lessons for educators in this present age of information are clear. It is important for us to help the children we teach not only to learn to access the information available but to know who controls that information, for information is power. They also need to appreciate that it can be transmitted and received around the world almost instantaneously.

Central to this control is the computer and it follows therefore that we should, if we wish to maintain our place in the world, have a computer literate population. This type of literacy will no doubt merge with other aspects of emergent literacy that have been mentioned already. Although this will take time to develop, its urgency is reinforced by the statistic concerning home computer ownership to which we have referred. Nonetheless, there is much to be done in schools to provide children with activities that will heighten their awareness of the computer's capabilities.

There is, also, a further asset to be added to the use of computers in school. This is its capability of supporting the language and language-related activities of our students. These will be illustrated in a number of ways during the suggestions for literacy teaching described in Chapters 6 and 7, where we will describe how the dynamics of the computer can bring alive the reading and writing processes.

We also wish to alert you to the way in which the computer can greatly assist you in the management of your group of learners, but we need first to give you an initial description of a method of monitoring children's reading progress. This will then become part of an overall management plan for ensuring reading progress.

Summary

This first chapter has attempted to give an overview of reading as it is thought of today. We have noted how the perspective has changed from one that has relied heavily on the psychology of perception to one that views reading as a language process. Learning how to read is now seen to be rooted in the social setting of the family, thus reflecting its level of literacy awareness. In this we have charted briefly the changes in thinking about language learning that have taken us from the viewpoint of separate mode (speaking, listening, reading and writing) development to one that is wholistic in its approach. Further, the development is thought of as emerging from the child's early years. These changes in viewpoints and perspectives together with the new technologies will, we suggest, have far-reaching implications for teaching.

CHAPTER 2

Changes in thinking about reading

Reading as a process

Before considering what is entailed when reading is viewed as a language process, it is necessary to record one other noticeable change in thinking. This is the change in emphasis from product to process in the study of both reading and writing. We have referred to reading and writing as processes so far, but it should be noted that it is only recently that the emphasis has moved from a concentration on the products of these skills to how reading and writing work. This means that educational researchers and other thinkers are no longer so concerned as they were with the end product, the composition or reading comprehension results, but more in the processes that operate in the construction of the products. This change in emphasis is welcome for it is the process that is, or should be, of greater concern to the teacher than the product. As was said elsewhere (Chapman, 1983), knowing about the process is crucial for this is where the teacher can intervene to improve the eventual product. Putting it in a nutshell you could say that process is more teaching oriented, and product is more assessment oriented. In this book we concentrate on process as guide to practice, and both product and process in those sections which deal with monitoring and assessment.

Reading as a language process

So far we have been relating how the study of language when applied to children's reading and writing has revealed certain implicit features that may account for some of the successes and failures of the teaching of reading. This recent thinking has signalled a considerable change in the way reading has been conceived by some researchers. As we have noted, the perspective has moved away from one that thought of reading mainly as a psychological perceptual process, which was largely concerned with visual perception, to one giving greater prominence to reading being part of an on-going language learning process.

In order to discuss systematically the language processing involved in reading, however, we need first to enunciate a theory of language that is sufficiently powerful and robust to embrace the factors introduced briefly in the first two chapters. Such a description will also provide the framework necessary for our purpose of rethinking reading, as well as enabling us to relate some aspects of the research reported in the next chapter. Some teachers may not be convinced of the need for a discussion of a theory of language in what is meant to be largely a practical analysis of reading development. This is particularly so as the following theory is difficult in the first place and we have little room to deal with it at length. However, we trust all will come to understand the necessity for such an input when we relate the complex set of language relationships involved in literacy teaching.

To perform their tasks adequately teachers need knowledge of the multitudinous factors associated with successful language and literacy learning. And, although there are many descriptions of language now available, only one, in our opinion, is sufficiently unified to account for the many aspects of literacy involved in education. This is the description provided by the linguist Michael Halliday who, with his wife Ruqaiya Hasan, has contributed so much that is both stimulating to teachers' thinking about literacy, and relevant to their classroom practice.

Some features of Halliday's description of language

Much of the prolific work of Halliday could be commented upon, especially as he is perhaps the one prominent linguist who has been consistently concerned with education, but that would be far beyond the scope of this part of the book. In order to appreciate how such a theory might account for some of the factors involved in learning to read and reading development, it is necessary first to outline very briefly some of the major principles of Halliday's description of language, which is sometimes called systemic linguistics. It must be stressed that what follows in no way attempts even an introduction to the theoretical stance of the systemic linguistics, but rather highlights some of the insights on reading and literacy teaching that they have provided.

Halliday's main tenets are that language is both a social and functional process. We have already introduced briefly some aspects of the social nature of language in Chapter 1, particularly those relating to the home and school, and here we spell out a little more of that social perspective.

As language evolved from the start for the purpose of communicating with our fellows, it will naturally have many direct relationships with the social environment in which it occurs. For example, children become members of groups, the family, playgroups, school classes and so on, and in these situations language is the principal method through which that membership is expressed. It is very important to note the implications of these language-social processes, for as we have noted the social aspects become, as does language, so internalized as to become opaque. They melt, as it were, into the background. However, for certain teaching purposes we need to reveal them so as to make use of them. For instance, children soon become able to adjust their language to the status of others in their group. This is revealed by the way they speak deferentially to the leader of the group or the Head teacher in the school. On the other hand, they are just as able to adjust their speech to the needs of the younger members of their group. It is surprising how expert the young language user is in this respect. We will mention these abilities again when we look at the appropriateness of language in different situations.

As we have noted, the account which follows is only a sketch of the description or model of language that Halliday and his co-workers have produced. We only attempt to give a flavour of the work and you are strongly recommended to go to the original sources to read further on this topic.

We have said that systemic linguistics, which is a branch of European linguistics, gives sociological aspects of language a high priority and views language as a form of 'doing' rather than 'knowing'. Further, it attempts to explain a number of aspects of language as clines. A 'cline', according to Berry (1977:26) 'is a scale on which all points shade into each other.' This concept can be applied in many ways where the data cannot be categorized as falling into black and white compartments. One example given is that of grammaticality. Systemic linguistics would not wish to decide whether a sentence was grammatical or not, as does transformational grammar, without reference to its social context. In this you may have been reminded of our earlier discussion which noted the extent of the variety of English in this country. So, as Berry suggests, 'A sentence might well be un-acceptable/unusual/unlikely in certain types of situation but acceptable/usual/likely in others.' This notion of the cline fits some aspects of language more readily than discrete categories. We make use of it later to describe reading where it is rarely a question of being able to read or not being able to read, but rather being able to read some texts fluently and others not so effectively.

Berry whose account we follow, also notes that with other linguists, systemic linguists attempt to verify their hypotheses by observing texts and by using statistical techniques. And finally for our purposes we record the notion of 'system', from whence systemic, which is central to this school of linguistics. A system in this sense is a category in a particular description of language, and is 'a set of linguistic options available in a certain environment'. In other terms, there is no one way of making meaning: the language provides a number of options from which the language user chooses.

Halliday agrees with most linguists that language is best characterized as a system of three layers:

meaning (called semantics by linguists)
grammar or syntax (called lexicogrammatical structure by Halliday)
sounds/writing (called phonemes/graphemes by linguists)

The lexicogrammatical system is organized by rank. Each rank is the place where different components are mapped on to each other. Berry explains rank order in the following manner:

> A rank scale, then, is a list of units arranged in order of their size. Like any other list of things arranged in order of size or status, it is a *hierarchy*.
>
> A rank scale is a special kind of hierarchy in which the relationship between adjacent units is the same all the way down the scale...
>
> This relationship is a 'consists of' relationship if one is thinking downwards along a scale, and a constituency relationship if one is thinking upwards along the scale. Each unit consists of members of the unit next below and each unit provides the constituents of the unit next above.
>
> In English, sentences consist of clauses, clauses consist of groups, groups consist of words, and words consist of morphemes. Morphemes act as the constituents of words, words act as constituents of groups, groups act as the constituents of clauses and clauses act as the constituents of sentences.

(Berry 1975:105)

The rank scale is shown in diagram form in Figure 1.

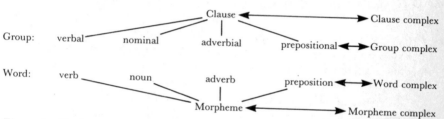

Figure 1   Rank scale for the lexicogrammar of English
After Halliday (1978:129)

We will be returning to the concept of rank scale in Chapter 4 when we provide the notion of reading ability being best conceived as a continuum or cline.

Learning how to mean: the functions of children's language

As well as being a social phenomenon language is also a functional one: the two are obviously closely associated, but what is meant by language being functional? Perhaps the clearest way to characterize it is to say that the functional approach to language attempts to identify what the user can *do* with it. To this end Halliday has identified seven ways by which children learn to use language as their language develops. These functions are said to be separate from each other or *monofunctional*. Halliday illustrates the way in which these develop by studying the early stages of his son Nigel's language. In his account of these (Halliday, 1975) he demonstrates well what he means by function, as he calls the process 'learning *how to* mean', which incidentally is also the title of his book. To emphasize the point he draws a clear distinction between 'acquiring a language' which implies that there is something out there to be got, and children learning language by actively making their own language and using it to mean and to learn.

The seven monofunctions of the child's language are:

Function	Example
Instrument	'I want'
Regulatory	'Do as I tell you'
Interaction	'Me and you'
Personal	'Here I come'
Heuristic	'Tell me why'
Imaginative	'Let's pretend
Representational	'I've got something to tell you'

These seven monofunctions become three *multifunctional* types as the child becomes an adult. And it should be noted here that, apart from the work of Halliday, there is little documentation of the transition from one system to the other.

After the early phases of language learning Halliday noticed that Nigel was employing intonation patterns, using rising tones for instrumental and regulatory functions, falling tones for personal or heuristic and both for the interactional function. It should be noticed that this is not according to adult intonation use but for contrast. However, Halliday believes that it leads to the abstract functional distinction of ideational and interpersonal functions of the adult system which is outlined below.

The functions of adult language

Halliday suggests that adult language contains three multifunctional components within the sematic, or meaning, component of language. (This you may recall was one of the three layers mentioned above that are agreed by most linguists.) He calls these the Ideational, the Interpersonal and the Textual (Halliday and Hasan 1976: 27). The Ideational component expresses 'content, what the language is about', the Interpersonal is concerned, as the name implies, with social, expressive and cognative functions, and the third component is the Textual or text-forming component of the system and it is this latter function that is of particular interest to the literacy teacher.

The textual component

The textual function, then, might inform us most about reading and to describe how the text is put together Halliday has proposed a text-forming component of the semantic or meaning system of language. This construct is rarely, if ever, met with in studies of reading. Considering the extent of interest there is in text processing and the comprehension of texts, it is strange that it has not been more to the fore as a theoretical framework for explaining text production and comprehending.

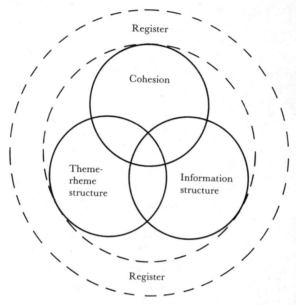

Figure 2   The text-forming component of the semantic system

As the diagram shows, the textual component comprises three sub-components: the theme/rheme or clause structure, the information system which signals the given/new distinction in the message and is carried by intonation and cohesion. This latter element, along with register, accounts for what Halliday has called the texture or textuality of a text. He uses the term to account for the phenomenon that makes us aware of the completeness and quality of a text. This becomes obvious when we look at a text and recognize that it is more than a collection of unrelated sentences and other linguistic features. Here we might use the Gestalt concept that the whole (text) is more than the some of its parts: it is this quality of wholeness that Halliday calls *texture*.

Summary of language functions

For an understanding of reading from a functional perspective, it is important to note that, for Halliday, text, be it spoken or written (he uses text to cover both modes), has a meaning function: a text is thereby a unit of meaning. In other words, to understand language from a functional perspective involves speaking of the language user making meaning, or, as we have seen, in terms of children learning their first language, they are learning how to mean. This, as will be readily appreciated, is an active approach that fits easily alongside the tradition in schools of learning through activity and experience. Language is considered to be for use: it is not something out there to be acquired, but it is by actively learning how to mean through the medium of language that the child learns to communicate. When considering reading this is an important new perspective which fits particularly well with some of the contemporary thinking we have already referred to, that is those who consider that reading is a 'meaning getting' process. When actively involved in reading, the reader is continually searching after meaning. But what are the other features predicted by the theory?

Cohesion

We turn now to one of the major topics of this book, and as it has so many implications and uses in teaching we will discuss it in greater detail.

The proposals for cohesion as set out by Halliday and Hasan (1976, 1980) have had a seminal effect on research. Many studies have been undertaken, many of them seeking, in various aspects of reading and writing, psychological relationships with those analysed as linguistic. We will be looking at a number of these in the sections that follow but now we will concentrate on how textual cohesion might be accommodated within the reading process.

Cohesion is said to be the means whereby items in a text, that are not otherwise accounted for by structural (that is basically syntactical) analysis, are linked together through their interdependence on one another for their interpretation. In other words, it is suggested that the meaning of one element, a word, a phrase, a clause or even a whole paragraph in a book cannot be totally understood in isolation. To be cohesive any one particular element has to be related to another for complete understanding. The term used by Halliday and Hasan (1976:3) to refer to a single instance of cohesion, the term for one occurrence of a pair of cohesively related items, is a *cohesive tie*. The ties are of different types and are grouped together according to the way they operate. You should note that for reading development we are interested in those cohesive ties that reach across the sentence boundary.

The constitutents of cohesion

It is important to notice at this point that since its first presentation in 1976, the description of texture, that is the combined effects of cohesion and register, has been extended and put more clearly into the context of Hallidayan functional grammar (Halliday and Hasan 1976 and 1980, Hasan 1984,

Halliday 1985). Some of these later clarifications form part of this explication.

Cohesive ties can be arranged in five groupings: *reference*, (pronouns like 'I', 'me', 'you', as well as 'this' and 'that'); *substitution* (e.g. the words, 'one', 'do', 'same', 'did it') and *ellipsis* (where the word or words are not physically present on the page but are understood from the previous context by the listener or reader); *conjunction* (for example the 'and', 'but', 'then' and 'so' words) and *lexical cohesion* (which arises through the author's choice of vocabulary). These original five have been reduced to four, substitution being subsumed by ellipsis (Halliday and Hasan, 1980).

Examples of cohesive ties

The following examples, which were selected by Eleanor Anderson, are taken from the reading survey materials of the Open University project on The Perception of Textual Cohesion. This project is discussed more fully in Chapter 4.

The lexical group

Halliday and Hasan propose two basic types of lexical tie. These are reiteration and collocation. Reiteration occurs when the same word is repeated; a near synonym is used, for example 'sorcerer' and 'wizard'; a superordinate, that is a general term which is related to specific terms, for example, 'flower' and 'tulip'; or a general noun like 'people'.

Collocation refers to words that regularly occur together. Common pairs of words like 'bread and butter' or 'mild and bitter' are said to be collocates. But it is not only these two word collocates; the language contains thousands of examples of groups of words that are more likely to co-occur statistically than other groups of words. We suggest that this is one of the features of language that assists the reader to predict. These habitual associations, however, are lexical, not grammatical, that is, syntactical.

(a)   Reiteration
It is also important that *milk* is put into clean bottles. Flies like drinking *milk*, and they carry diseases (repetition of the word 'milk').

(b)   Collocation
Those with *gold* coins were to be the Rulers, called Guardians; those with *silver* ones were to make up the army, police and civil service, called Auxiliaires, and those with *iron* or *bronze* coins were to work providing food and other basic needs for the community. (The cohesion of the paragraph relies largely on the association of the words 'gold', 'silver', 'iron' and 'bronze'.)

The reference group

(a)   Personal

Plato was a Greek philosopher, born in 427 B.C. *His* idea was called 'The Republic'. *He* invented a Foundation Myth which explains why the country was to be divided into three kinds of people.

(b)   Demonstrative

In wet weather *you might get stuck*. Men working on a building site have *this* problem, so they build their own simple railway. (This is an example of one element consisting of four words being cohesively related to one word 'this'.)

(c)   Comparative

From the Masters and from ancient lore-books Ged learned what he could do about such beings as this *shadow* he had loosed: little was there to learn. No *such* creature was described or spoken of directly.

The substitution group

(a)   Nominal

Some car parts wear out. New *ones* must be fitted.

(b)   Verbal

All the animals in this book *feed their young with milk*. Animals which *do this* are mammals. (Here the words, 'feed their young with milk' is related to 'do this'.)

(c)   Clausal

I said, 'Yeah, that's right,' and he said, 'Well, now *you'll be signing full pro*.' 'I hope *so*,' I said, although I must admit it encouraged me, hearing Mike say that, because normally he didn't give anything away, old Mike. (Here the clause, 'you'll be signing full pro' is cohesively linked by 'so')

The ellipsis group
(In these examples the point where the ellipsis occurs is marked by *).

(a)   Nominal

He next looked the *pieces* over very carefully. Some of them were no use at all, but some * were long and thin.

(b)   Verbal

Rover set out to find if the gas turbine could *be adapted* to a motor car. It could * and it was * and in 1952, the Rover JET 1 set up the first officially recognized international speed records for turbine-powered cars.

(c)   Clausal
Which oxide of carbon have you made?
How did you tell *?

The conjunction group

(a)   Additive
The sticks grew into a skeleton. *And* before the farmer had started to give it flesh. Jan cried out, 'A canoe!'

(b)   Adversative
Often a cheap microscope is shaped to look like an expensive one in a laboratory. *But* lenses are far more important than outward appearances.

(c)   Causal
'Damsel,' answered Beaumains politely, 'you can say to me what you wish, but never will I turn back. *For* I have promised King Arthur to undertake your adventure – and achieve it I will, or die in the attempt.

(d)   Temporal
Once all the boxes are there they are opened, and the papers mixed together so that it is no longer possible to tell from which box they came. *Then* the count can begin.

Further examples of these groups of ties drawn from children's reading books will be found in Chapman (1983). And a more detailed explanation will be found in Halliday and Hasan, 1976).

Cohesive ties are said to form chains through a text and Anderson (1983) suggested that *co-reference* is the method used by authors to keep track of people, objects and places in a text. This he attributes to the chaining of reference and ellipsis/substitution cohesive ties. *Co-extension* is the selection of lexical items for a particular context and purpose and is carried by chains of lexical cohesive ties. *Conjoining*, the way parts of the text are logically related, is achieved, as the name implies, by the conjunction cohesive ties.

This then is part of a linguistic description of cohesion but in order to use this system of ties for a survey of reading in schools and for other research, it is necessary to know the detailed working of the cohesive tie itself. As you will realize it is also this kind of knowledge that is most useful for teaching. Cohesion is said to operate according to the principle of presupposition.

Presupposition

Presupposition is said to be the way in which cohesion is created in texts. And it is through this mechanism that the linguistic description has, we suggest, psychological implications. Halliday suggests that to achieve a cohesive effect some element in the text presupposes another so that the two elements, the presupposing and the presupposed, and thereby, at least potentially, integrated into the text.

Presupposition in the sense used here can be related to recent thinking in the study of reading because it goes a long way to explain the process of prediction or anticipation that comprises a large part of the reading process. In essence readers on perceiving the onset of a cohesive tie know, not only from the content (which is related to the top-down factor of the reading process we mentioned earlier), but from their knowledge of the language, that the other end of the tie will inevitably follow. This is regardless of the distance in terms of words, sentences or even paragraphs that separate the beginning and end of the tie. It is proposed therefore that the ability of readers to tie the tie, or effect tie closure, is an important concomitant of reading fluency. Those of you who are familiar with psychology will realize that these linguistic proposals will involve such psychological features as short-term or 'working' memory.

Chaining

An illustration of how this works can be taken from the personal reference system. Normally, the names to which a pronoun refers, the antecedents, are announced first, at the beginning of a story. Readers are primed by their knowledge of the pronoun system in English to anticipate that a person thus named will be referred to thereafter mostly be pronouns. These pronouns and other cohesive items can be likened to the links of a chain which help the text to hang together. It is proposed that the perception of the links (the pronouns ties in this case) enables readers to keep track of people, things or events in a text. It is clear again that this tracking involves a further cognitive element in addition to the closing, or tying, of a tie mentioned earlier. For example, in a fairy story the participants often change as the story proceeds, yet the pronoun remains exactly the same word. This is particularly noticeable with plurals like 'they' where readers need to constantly up-date the constitution of the group to which 'they' refers. It may be a boy and a girl who together set out on an adventure to be joined shortly by a dog or another character. And, as the story progresses the group, still referred to as 'they', is increased or decreased. It is suggested that this chaining of the ties provides a patterned pathway through the story. The tracking, or monitoring needed to keep to the path is provided by the reader. The processes of anticipation of tie closure and the tracking of the cohesive chains which are derived from the linguistic base are seen then to be inevitably associated with psychological factors during reading.

The other cohesive tie grouping have the same basic mechanism as co-reference, but co-extension and conjoining work slightly differently.

Co-extension is carried in the main by lexical cohesion or the author's vocabulary choice. Here the notion is that words that have close associative relationships are more likely to co-occur (be presupposed) in the same text environment than others that have little or no associative force. If the topic concerns avalanches, words like 'snow' and 'ice' are more likely to co-occur than words directly related to another topic, say cooking, although, as always in discussions about language there is frequently the possibility of metaphorical extensions. In linguistic terms, lexically cohesive words are said to be collocated, but this linguistic term implies much more than the presence of the simple word associations noted earlier. Some collocations are phrases that are frequently used and are so predictable and their force so great that beginning readers often give them prominence over the words that actually appear on the page. (You will find some examples of these in the profiling system outlined in a later chapter.) In order to use the cohesive tie system in research, the lexical chains, which might be otherwise over-subjectively judged, are analysed as chain links by Hasan (Halliday and Hasan 1980) only when they satisfy certain semantic relationships. These are synonymy, words that have nearly the same meaning; antonymy, words that are opposites; hyponymy, the relationship between an overall term and a subordinate; and meronomy, the part – whole relationship. Examples of these four are:

synonyms: 'sound', 'noise'; 'sour', 'tart'; 'marvel', 'wonder'.
antonyms: 'master', 'servant'; 'hovel', 'palace'; 'silly', 'sensible'.
hyponyms: 'flower', 'daisy'; 'vegetable', 'marrow'; 'class', 'pupil'.
meronomy: 'engine', 'sparking-plug'; 'hand', 'finger'; 'aeroplane', 'wings'.

There are differences also in the way that the conjoining cohesive ties work. They share the same basic presupposition mechanism but do not perform in quite the same way. The conjoining ties indicate, or clearly specify, ways in which the meaning relations expressed by the clauses are systematically connected with what has gone before. Sometimes the logic of the meaning carried by the clause structures allows their junction to be implicit; sometimes the conjunction cohesive tie is used to confirm the nature of that junction; sometimes it specifies the meaning connection very clearly indeed. Originally, four areas of meaning relations were covered by these ties, additive, adversative, temporal and causal. These were revised and extended more recently by Halliday (1985).

Genre and register

The term genre has a long history in literary studies and you may have come across it in such discussions. Recently, however, the term has been used to cover the whole range of language production both oral and written. Christie (1984), for example, uses it to refer to 'any purposeful, staged, cultural activity'. One important consideration that Halliday has consistently maintained is the importance of the context of any langauge event. Any piece of text, he maintains, is produced in some setting and can only be understood fully when that situation and the purpose that gave it birth is known. This being so, part of the reading process must, therefore, entail the perception of context and response to the author's purposes in writing the text.

It is obvious that there are many different genres to which children will be introduced as they go through their schooling. They will meet and read many stories, information books, instructions of various types, descriptions or expository texts and so on: each having a different purpose. And the important point to notice is that these genres differ from each other linguistically according to their contexts. It has been suggested by the systemic linguists that these contexts can be described by using the concept of register. This notion is concerned with the relationship of the text with its context. In Hallidayan terms registers are not marginal or just special varieties of language: they cover between them the total range of language activity.

It was noted earlier that the concept of cohesion was closely related to that of register. These two are said to account for the 'texture of text'. Unlike cohesion, which is concerned with the internal unity of the text, register, as we have noted, accounts for the relationship of the text to its context. You will recall that we noted earlier in this chapter how Halliday laid great store as to the importance of the notion of the variety of language being appropriate to the situation in which it was being used. Register then, is that property of text that signals the appropriateness of the text to the situation of its existence. In schools the major register difference, after the basic differences between speaking and writing, is between fiction and non-fiction. Many of the register distinctions within the factual texts are to do with the subject textbooks. As you will read in the research review that follows there is some evidence that cohesion varies according to the style of the writer (Gutwinski 1976) and according to academic subject (Blinkley 1983).

There are three features, or clines, that are used to identify a register: its field of discourse, its tenor and its mode. Pearce, quoted in Halliday (1978:33) summarizes these as follows:

Field refers to the institutional setting in which a piece of language occurs and embraces not only the subject matter in hand but the whole activity of the speaker or participant in a setting (we might add 'and of the other participant'...)

Tenor... refers to the relationship between the participant...not merely variation in formality... but... such questions as the permanence or otherwise of the relationship and the degree of emotional charge in it...

Mode refers to the channel of communication adopted: not only the choice between spoken and written medium, but much more detailed choices (we might add: 'and other choice relating to the role of language in the situation' ...)

Gregory and Carrol (1978:9) point out that using these three clines enables us to make predictions about the language that might be used in certain situations. They say:

Many texts can be located roughly on the clines field, mode and tenor. For example, 'lectures (modes and tenors) on geography (field)', 'sermons (field, mode and tenors)', 'cooking (field) recipe (tenors) books (mode)', 'personal (field and tenor) conversation (tenor and mode)'.

Benson and Greaves (1973:71–81) illustrate the way in which certain words or word complexes predict the field of discourse. They use two examples, one to do with weather and weather forecasting and another with sociology. They show that the former is marked most strongly by vocabulary and the type of print used. In this latter, the text on sociology, they show how the field and its subfields are delimited by the scientific nature of the vocabulary.

It is interesting to note how certain words in a text, the nouns, verbs, adjectives and adverbs (which are called lexical items by linguists), indicate the genre of the text. For example, if the word 'astronaut' is met early in a text, you will be alerted and anticipate the other associated words will follow. You would not be surprised to read words like 'rocket', 'space' and 'weightlessness'. As you read on, you will begin to establish the register of the text and this would enable you to make further predictions as to the context and the author's meaning. (Sets of words from the cohesion project materials will be found in Appendix 3. Cover one of the lists and try to guess the topic by uncovering the first word only. Then predict some of the words that might follow. Continue to uncover the rest of the list to confirm your prediction.)

It follows, therefore, that children must become sensitive to register and must be able to predict that which is fitting, language-wise, in any particular situation. Moreover, it is suggested that these features of register can be used to describe, and distinguish between, that vast range of texts found in schools, from those that are used in the infant school for the teaching of reading to those that are studied for school leaving examinations.

The study of genre and register, particularly in the way we have outlined, is in its early stages only and we are a long way from being able to list the many genre and their register distinctions. However, work is proceeding, particularly in Australia where these features have been introduced to teachers through the distance teaching courses produced by Deakin University.

Summary of cohesion and register

Cohesion, or text unity, is a global quality of text that operates within an appropriate register. It is accounted for by a series of interlocking linguistic features, the cohesive ties, which indicate the meaning relations that exist within local areas of the text. Many of these ties are chained so as to keep track of people, objects and events. Others, which are charged with associative values, form lexical chains. The conjoining cohesive ties indicate or confirm a series of logical or other meaning relationships. All operate by a process called presupposition and must be perceived within a variety of registers which, together with the monitoring processes involved by the chaining system, make up a part of the reading process.

CHAPTER 3

A decade of reading research

It is possible within the confines of this volume to mention only briefly the vast amount of research into reading that has taken place in the previous 10 years. Indeed, such has been the amount undertaken that we have had to make a further restriction and cite only that research that appears to have direct relevance to classroom teaching. However, in making this selection we have indicated what we consider to be important and have given references to further reading.

It is important to be aware that the advances made in reading research during recent years have been extensive. Although we have still a great deal to learn, there is a more optimistic view, in some countries, than one would gather from some recent comments in this country.

Take, for example, this statement,

> Little is known about the processes that underlie efficient reading. No one model of the reading process is generally accepted to be an adequate representation of the process by which readers understand what they read.
>
> (Gorman 1986:5)

This is the opening statement of the section on the Assessment of Reading and part of the framework or rationale for the construction of the assessment materials by the Assessment of Performance Unit which is monitoring reading nationally. Whilst it is true that our knowledge is incomplete, it is strange to find that much highly relevant research that has been done, particularly in other countries, appears to have been ignored by the assessment team.

When this is compared with the recent publication in the United States of America of the Report of the Commission on Reading, 'Becoming a Nation of Readers', the contrast is stark indeed. In the introduction we find this statement:

> The last two decades of research and scholarship on reading, building on the past, have produced an array of information which is unparalleled in its understanding of the underlying processes in the comprehension of language. Although reading abilities and disabilities require further investigation, present knowledge, combined

with the centrality of literacy in the educational process, make the report one for optimism. Gains from reading research demonstrate the power of new spectra of research findings and methodologies to account for the cognitive activities entailed in school learning. And because, in the schools and classrooms across the country, reading is an essential tool for success, we can hope for significant advances in academic achievement as the policies and practices outlined in these pages become more widespread.

(Glaser 1985:viii)

At least this Report tells us that there is more agreement about what reading is in the United States! The authors state:

Substantial evidence in understanding the process of reading have been made in the last decade. The majority of the scholars in the field now agree on the nature of reading: Reading is the process of constructing meaning from texts. It is a complex skill requiring the coordination of a number of interrelated sources of information.

Reading can be compared to the performance of a symphony orchestra. This analogy illustrates three points. First, like the performance of a symphony, reading is a wholistic act. In other words, while reading can be analysed into subskills such as discriminating letters and identifying words, performing the subskills one at a time does not constitute reading. Reading can be said to take place only when the parts are put together in a smooth, integrated performance. Second, success in reading comes from practice over long periods of time, like skill in playing musical instruments. Indeed, it is a lifelong endeavour. Third, as with a musical score, there may be more than one interpretation of a text. The interpretation depends upon the background of the reader, the purpose for reading, and the context in which reading occurs.

(Anderson *et al.* 1985:7)

We relate next some of the research that has been carried out in this and other countries, particularly that which gives rise to the optimism referred to above. In order to organize this review we have divided it into sections according to the perspective adopted by the researchers.

Reading research from a psychological perspective

We begin this very brief review of recent developments in reading research by looking first at reading from a psychological perspective. In this we give pride of place to reading's crucial importance to thinking. Donaldson (1978), to whom we referred earlier, has written about the effect reading has on the developing mind. In this, it is very nature of the written word that has, it would seem, a far-reaching effect. The written word is unlike speech or conversation between two or more people as it is not taking place in the here and now where the setting, or context, is obvious to both parties. In speech, as we noted earlier, some of the meaning is conveyed by intonation, as in a question where the sounds of the words follow a rising tone. A certain amount is conveyed also by gesture and in other non-verbal ways. But more important for the point being made here is in the context in which the conversation is taking place as this, in itself, is a part of the meaning being transmitted. Items in a room, for example, can be referred to without words actually being used to name and describe them. These factors, together with the ephemeral nature of speech, all add up to the fact that speech leaves little choice of meaning. In written language, however, the actual physical context is not available and the author has to replace it by providing the reader with a context. In this respect, the author expects readers to infer the meaning not only from the clues given by the text but from their own background knowledge of similar situations with which they are familiar. Although writing only provides a little of the richness of the context of speech nonetheless it has one very important characteristic: it is not ephemeral, it makes language visible and permanent. This permanence is most important for it enables the reader to consider language as an *object*, and so become aware of the different possibilities as to what the text means. Because of its significance we repeat the quote from Donaldson:

> Thus it turns out that those very features of the written word which encourage awareness of language may also encourage awareness of one's own thinking and be relevant to the development of intellectual control, with incalculable consequences for the development of the kinds of thinking which are characteristic of logic, mathematics and the sciences.
>
> (Donaldson 1978:95)

While the relationship drawn by Donaldson between reading and the written word is persuasive, it does not have everyone's agreement and we report below the alternative views of some sociologists and anthropologists. But for the moment we continue with research from a psychological viewpoint.

Schema research

Comprehension and the retention in memory of what has been read has been a central concern of the psychology of reading for many years. And recently there have been significant developments in three areas in particular. These advances are concerned with the notions of schema, metacognition and text structure. It is with the former that a link can be made with Donaldson's discussion of the relationship between reading and thinking.

Although Donaldson does not refer to research on schemata that has been carried out in the United States, developments there have thrown light on the nature of the effects of the reader's background knowledge on their reading comprehension.

From the work that has been done it is clear that a certain level of background knowledge, or prior knowledge as it is sometimes called, is required to understand an author's meaning. This knowledge is said to be stored in memory in *schemata* and in referring to it we follow the account given by Anderson and Pearson (1984). Although it is only possible to give a brief sketch here you should be aware that considerable advances have been made in our understanding of the reading process as a result of this work.

The schema theorists follow the work of Bartlett (1932) and the earlier Gestalt psychologists, who see understanding as an interaction between existing knowledge already stored in memory with new knowledge being gained from the text. In these terms comprehension could be stated as being a synthesis of old and new information.

A schema is an abstract knowledge structure that holds a summary of what is known about a particular topic in memory, in this case (Figure 3) 'Making a plane journey'. This abstraction is akin to what many would call a concept and it is built up of numerous experiences of the entity in question so that its essential characteristics are distilled from a large number of particular instances. For example, children devleop a schema for animals from the experience of many animals which differ in their individual particulars. Children are soon able to categorize an animal as such, being aware that it is alive and so on.

The advances made in this area have come from computer scientists and their simulations of human cognition or the creation of artificial intelligences. You may recall that we noted also that the interactive model of the reading process has come from this developing science.

One of the most important processes in schema-theoretic accounts is our ability to draw differences. In this process the reader often goes beyond the author's meaning. Anderson and Pearson (1984:269) outline four types of inferencing that have been researched. In comprehending these are:

1. Deciding what schema among many should be called into play.
2. Instantiating slots within a selected schema. That is, providing an entity not actually mentioned but inferred.
   ['Instantiation' is a technical term in this theory and refers to the filling of the slots in schemata with particular cases, a process considered critical for active comprehension.]
3. Assigning default values. That is, filling in a slot with no substantial information.
4. Drawing a conclusion based upon lack of knowledge.

(Anderson and Pearson 1984:269)

Summing up some of the work they now feel able to state:

available data support the ideas that the reader's schema is a structure that facilitates planful retrieval of text information from memory and permits reconstruction of elements that were not learned or have been forgotten.

(Anderson and Pearson 1984:285)

A large amount of this research has been done at 'The Center for the Study of Reading' at the University of Illinois in the United States of America. And although there is much more research to be done, it is obvious from the results so far reported that much has been achieved in unravelling some of the intricate problems relating to comprehension.

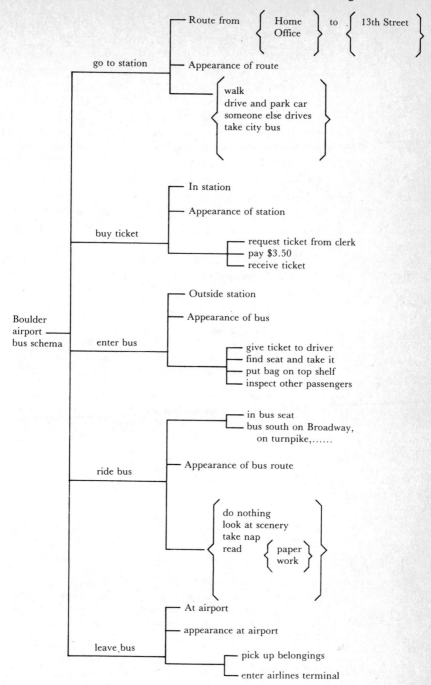

Figure 3 An example of a schema
After Kintsch (1977:376)

Metacognition

Flavell (1978) defined metacognition as 'knowledge that takes as its object or regulates any aspect of any cognitive endeavour'. However, the term metacognition has been used to discuss two different types of phenemenon. The two elements are knowledge about cognition and regulation of cognition. Baker and Brown (1984), whose review of metacognitive skills and reading we are following, referring to the first of these, state that 'The ability to reflect on ones activities when reading, solving problems, and so on, is a late-developing skill with important implications for the child's effectiveness as an active, planful learner.' It follows that if a child knows what is needed to perform effectively, then, on reaching that later development, improvement can be expected to become independent. The second phenomenon is said to consist of self-regulatory mechanisms such as checking, planning, monitoring and evaluating how one learns.

Metacognition is a complex area about which a great deal of research has taken place. In order to give a flavour of it, we use the same quote as Baker and Brown use when discussing work on comprehension monitoring:

> A good reader proceeds smoothly and quickly as long as his understanding of the material is complete. But as soon as he senses that he has missed an idea, that the track has been lost, he brings smooth progress to a grinding halt. Advancing more slowly, he seeks clarification in the subsequent material, examining it for the light it can throw on the earlier trouble spot. If still dissatisfied with his grasp, he returns to the point where the difficulty began and rereads the section more carefully. He probes and analyses the sentences for their exact meaning; he tries to visualize abstruse descriptions; and through a series of approximations, deductions, and corrections he translates scientific and technical terms into concrete examples.
>
> (Whimbey 1975:91)

We will be referring again to metacognition in Chapter 5.

Text structure

The text structuralists have attempted to show that there are features of the organization of a text that have a direct bearing on how that text is understood and remembered. Meyer and Rice claim that these studies show that:

> First, text structure is a significant dimension along which text selections can be evaluated as to their similarities and differences. Second, specifying the text structure allows the researcher to identify the amount and type of information which readers remember from text. Third, it allows variations that may arise between the text and the reader's understanding of the text.
>
> (Meyer and Rice 1984:319)

The term 'proposition' is often used in text structure research. It is defined as a 'thought unit containing a relation, or attribute, and an argument'. Again you would need to know how some of those terms are used so we give examples of propositions instead of a series of further definitions.

The following is a short extract from the work of Kintsch (1977):

> ... the meaning of a text is its text base. The text base consists of a sequence of propositions; propositions are in turn composed of concepts. Each proposition consists of one relational term and one or more arguments. For instance, consider the proposition (HIT, GEORGE, JOHN) in the figure below. It consists of three concepts, the relation HIT and the arguments GEORGE and JOHN.

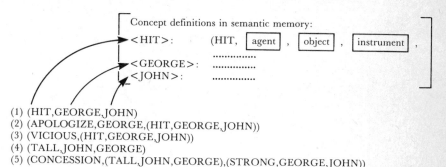

(1) (HIT,GEORGE,JOHN)
(2) (APOLOGIZE,GEORGE,(HIT,GEORGE,JOHN))
(3) (VICIOUS,(HIT,GEORGE,JOHN))
(4) (TALL,JOHN,GEORGE)
(5) (CONCESSION,(TALL,JOHN,GEORGE),(STRONG,GEORGE,JOHN))

Figure 4 Examples of propositions
After Kintsch (1977:343)

It is suggested that text structure can be analysed at three levels. The sentence is seen as the first or micropropositional level and the paragraph as the second or macropropositional level. The former assists the text to cohere and the latter accounts for issues of organization and argumentation. The third level is the top-level structure of the text as a whole.

Meyer and Rice (1984) suggest that cohesion operates at the first or micropropositional level. There is also mention of logical and rhetorical relations at the macropropositional level and the work of Halliday to which we have already referred in Chapter 2.

One type of text structure that has been developed, and that we will use as an example, is story grammar. In this the organization of a story is built up by a set of rewrite rules (see Figure 5) like those of transformational grammar. The significant features of the grammar are settings, episodes and events. And as you will appreciate, these rules apply not to one particular story but to any story.

A number of other ways of analysing text structures have been put forward and because of the detail required each method is very time consuming to undertake.

Although there is a great deal more to be done, this line of research has shown that it is possible to predict from the structure of the text which ideas will be recalled and how long it will take readers to study a text.

Some of the research referred to above has been well reviewed in the *Handbook of Reading Research* (Pearson *et al.* 1984) and those seeking more detail should consult that authoritative source.

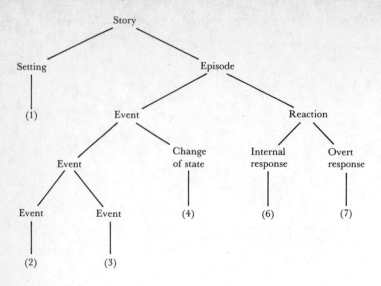

Figure 5   The syntactic structure of the story
(from Rumelhart: 1975)

Reading research from a psychological perspective

Although a considerable amount of research of a psycholinguistic nature has been carried out, especially following the publication of the generative transformational grammar by Chomsky (Chomsky 1957, 1965), we concentrate here on the work of Goodman whose model of the reading process used Chomsky's insights for his theory. We looked at this briefly as an illustration of top-down processing in the previous chapter. For some unknown reason this work is not featured in the *Handbook of Research in Reading* although it has made a considerable impact on the teaching of reading and it is for this reason that it has been selected here.

The research data that Goodman has collected have been analysed according to a system called *miscue analysis*. This procedure involves noting carefully children's oral reading of a text and recording their mistakes, hesitations, self-corrections and substitutions. Goodman prefers to call these *miscues* rather than errors. The miscues are analysed according to the linguistic features that gave rise to them. That is, Goodman has shown that they can be traced to their positions in the text according to whether their origins are syntactical, semantic or phonographic.

The importance of Goodman's research lies in its acceptance by many teachers as a way of making their listening to children's reading more effective. It is claimed that, by mentally carrying out a miscue analysis as they listen to reading, teachers are thereby better able to build up their children's strengths. The method has had a boost in this country recently as a result of the research of Southgate *et al.* (1981) where the use of miscue analysis is recommended to enhance the teaching of reading.

Reading research from a sociolinguistic perspective

The very term 'socio' when discussing the study of language is virtually redundant for, as we have seen, language is inextricably tied to social functions. The study of reading from such a perspective, therefore, will touch on areas already mentioned. In their summary of this, Bloom and Green (1984:415) stress the importance of context in reading, as it is embedded in both an intrapersonal (within the person) and interpersonal (between persons) context. This is shown by the ways that teachers structure the settings of reading and the ways in which students use language in their interactions. Among the other points listed, they agree that 'literacy learning is a process of gradual socialization to print, which can be supported by formal and informal contexts for literacy in classrooms and other settings.' (ibid:415)

There is, as we indicated earlier, a challenge to the relationship between reading and thinking that is claimed by some psychologists. This challenge arises from sociological and anthropoligical studies where claims for the advantageous effects of literacy on higher cognitive processes are disputed. The forces that are at work during language and literacy education, they propose, are forms of socialization into the ways of the main stream culture. In a very useful 'Review Article' on the topic, Gee, an American writer, points out that:

> Different societies and social subgroups have different types of literacy, and literacy has different social and cultural contexts. Literacy is seen as a set of discourse practices, that is, as ways of using language and making sense in both speech and writing. These discourse practices are tied to the particular world views (beliefs and values) of particular social or cultural groups. Such discourse practices are integrally connected with the identity or sense of self of the people who practise them; a change of discourse practices is a change of identity.
>
> The discourse practices associated with our schools represent the world view of mainstream and powerful institutions in our society; these discourse practices and their concomitant world view are necessary for social and economic success in our society.
>
> (Gee 1986:720)

Writings and research from this perspective illustrate that there is no link between literacy acquisition and higher mental skills like analytic and logical or abstract thinking as Miller and Donaldson suggest. As Gee puts it, 'All humans who are acculturated and socialized are already in possession of higher order cognitive skills, though their expression and the practices they are embedded in will differ across cultures.' (ibid:721)

However, while there is no denying the strengths of these thoughts and findings, it remains the job of teachers to help children acquire the literacy of the main culture, and this in itself requires those higher order thinking skills.

Future instructional research

In order to summarize this section of selected reports, we quote again from Anderson and Pearson (1984), who suggest some problems that need further elucidation for instruction.

> First, poor readers are likely to have gaps in knowledge. Since what a person already knows is a principal determiner of what she can comprehend, the less she knows the less she can comprehend.
> Second, poor readers are likely to have an impoverished understanding of the relationships among the facts they do not know about a topic. Arbitrary information is a source of confusion, slow learning, slow processing, and unsatisfactory reasoning.
> Third, poor readers are unlikely to make the inference required to weave the information given in a text into a coherent overall representation. Poor readers do not seem consistently to appreciate that ... comprehending a story or text is like completing a jigsaw puzzle; all the information must be used, the information must fit into place without forcing, all of the important slots must contain information, and the completed interpretation must make sense.
>
> (Anderson and Pearson 1984:286)

We move on now to review research that has been prompted by the publication of Halliday and Hasan (1976) on cohesion. We give more details of this as it is likely to become a very important body of knowledge for teachers.

Cohesion research related to reading

In Chapter 2 we outlined Halliday's description of language, noting particularly the concept of texture. This we learned consisted of two factors, those of cohesion and genre or register. We look next, in a little more detail than we have been able to do with other areas, at the research that has been undertaken using Halliday and Hasan's (1976) proposals for cohesion in English. We list each work according to the researcher who reported it. You may find it necessary to refer back to Chapter 2 to refresh your memory of the details of their system of cohesive ties.

Before we relate these studies, and so that you will understand the research more readily and fully, we give first the meaning of a few terms with which you may not be familiar.

The terms are 'anaphoric', 'cataphoric', 'exophoric', 'cloze procedure' and 'readability formulae'.

The linguistic term 'anaphoric' refers to the way in which one element, usually a word, say a pronoun, refers back to another, often a name, or noun or another pronoun. This is often compared with the term 'cataphoric' or forward acting reference, where the pronoun precedes the name or noun.

The term exophoric is a reference term also; it is used to indicate the way in which a word or words in a text refers to the outside, or nonlinguistic context, for a full interpretation. The identity of 'he' for example, in the song 'for he's a jolly good fellow' is undoubtedly known to those present but not to us. This exophoric reference is common in the early writing of children.

Cloze procedure is a technique, which, as you will read later, was strongly advocated by Lunzer and Gardner (1979) as a basis for the discussion of texts by children. In its traditional form it consists of the deletion of words at regular intervals, the reader being expected to replace the omitted words. There are now many variations of the traditional version which was claimed to both act as a measure of the text's readability and of the reader's comprehension ability. It has been suggested that its strength lies in that it reflects the reader's interaction with the text whereas other measures like readability formulae do not. You will find a chapter on cloze procedure in Chapman (1983).

The measurement of a text's readability, whether it is more or less difficult for particular purposes, by formulae, is, at first sight, very attractive. The basic formulae, and there are many, use word frequency, word length and average sentence length as the most significant predictors of difficulty. The formulae are easy to calculate, particularly since the introduction of microcomputers to schools, and give a semblance of objectivity. They have, however, been heavily criticized for being too simplistic in that they do not take important reading characteristics, like reader interest, into consideration. As noted, unlike cloze they do not reflect the interaction of the reader with the text.

A further point raised in one of the research summaries is the notion of 'tie distance'. That is, the distance in terms of intervening sentence between the onset of a tie and its closure. If the closing end of a tie is in the following sentence, the tie is termed 'immediate'. If it is one or more sentences distant, it is termed 'remote', and if there is a further tie within the distance, it is 'mediated'.

Before presenting summaries of the research pertinent to the school situation we relate, for interest, some of the work that has been done using cohesion analysis in vastly different fields.

One of the first to apply cohesion analysis to written texts was Gutwinski (1976) who showed how the framework of cohesion may be used in the study of literary style. He applied the analysis system to passages from Ernest Hemingway and Henry James. His work demonstrated quite clearly that cohesion analysis applied to written text can differentiate between authors' styles.

Rochester and Martin (1979) used cohesion research to investigate the discourse failure of schizophrenics. They examined the discourse of three groups; thought disordered patients, non-thought disordered patients and normal speakers, in two situations, interview and narrative. Their results indicated that the schizophrenic patients were able to recognize differences in context quite clearly. They differed however in two ways. They relied less on cohesion in narrative than normal speakers and thought disordered speakers relied more on lexical cohesion in interviews than non-disordered patients. The researchers report that 'the two measures of cohesion were highly sensitive to context differences and only moderately sensitive to differences among groups'.

One further study of general interest is that carried out by Esau (1982) of the so called 'smoking gun tape', one of the released Watergate tapes. Through a careful analysis of cohesion devices – reference, substitution, ellipsis and lexical chaining – he demonstrated an unusual amount of ambiguity and vagueness in the tape compared with the 'backstage' conversations recorded. He pointed out that 'cohesion devices have both a uniting and a separating function; they do not merely tie together discrete utterances into a continuous text, but they also serve to erect a partition between insiders and outsiders to a conversation'.

We now go on to give short reviews of some of the research that has been done using the concepts of cohesion and register for educational purposes. Firstly, we note that a number of studies has been carried out that indicate some of the factors associated with cohesion as part of general language development. Garber (1979) compared selective cohesive features in the language produced by six five-year-old children, three boys and three girls, with those in their beginning reading materials. The children, who came from middle-class backgrounds had had the same kindergarten experience and had been judged by their teachers to be able to succeed in the first year reading programme. They were further judged to be at least of average intelligence and had had no apparent language problems. The children participated in a total of six language situations so that the researcher could collect a wide range of their oral language. She found that this child-produced language contained each of the five groups of cohesive ties proposed by Halliday and Hasan but that not every type of tie was found in the three reading books selected. This interesting study is one of the few that presents evidence of cohesion in early oral language.

Rhodes (1979) studied the predictability of four simple stories which reflected differing models of reading instruction. Using retelling of the stories as her method of gauging effects, she found a persistent relationship between the types of reading material and the children's reading behaviour. She found significant correlations between the results of analysis by story structure and cohesion. She found that the analysis provided some differences between more and less predictable texts. In the study readability formulae are said not to have predicted difficulty.

Moberly (1978) noted that earlier research into anaphoric cohesion was limited to reference types, with personal pronouns being studied the most. However, the results of this earlier work were inconsistent. Moberly investigated the ability of 10 and 12 year olds to identify four types of anaphoric relations in the three tie locations, remote, mediated and immediate. She used two stories in her research asking children to write down the presupposed item next to its underlined anaphoric form. Her results showed that all three variables, age, anaphoric type and location produced significant differences in performance. She also found significant differences between the mean scores of reference and ellipsis types. She reports that the distance between the ties and their type had an important effect on performance as did the age of the children.

Monson (n.d.) using four samples, totalling 230 children aged from 7 to 12 years, investigated the comprehension of anaphoric relationships in forward and backward (pointing) positions. She used four short stories to test the understanding of each type of cohesion (pronoun-referent, lexical, substitution/ellipsis) in anaphoric and cataphoric positions. In all instances one end of a cohesive tie was separated from the other by at least one sentence, that is, they were remote.

The method used was one in which the children were asked 'to read the stories first, then locate the first underlined word and find another word or group of words in the story that it referred to'. They were instructed 'to draw a line around the word or words and extend the line to the underlined words'. The children were reported as having no difficulty with the procedure.

Monson's studies indicate significant growth in the understanding of reference structures between 7 and 8 years, of substitution/ellipsis structures between 9 and 10 years, and of cataphoric ties between 8 and 9 years of age. She adds that the development of anaphoric comprehension appears to move rather slowly during the elementary or primary years. Only about three-quarters of the referent items were understood by 11 and 12 year olds in the study. The results for lexical and substitution/ellipsis items were even lower than the referent items, with two-thirds of the lexical items and only one-half of the substitution/ellipsis items being understood by any age group.

In a study of 74 eight-year-old fluent and non-fluent readers, Chapman (1979a) demonstrated that the perception of cohesive ties was significantly related to reading fluency.

Chapman and Stokes (1980) investigated developmental trends in the perception of cohesion using a modified cloze procedure. Three groups of children, aged 8, 11 and 14 years, were asked to replace pronouns, conjunctions and non-pronouns in 14 stories. Significant correlations were found between chronological age with pronoun and conjunction scores. The results indicated a developmental pattern of mastery over the three deletion types.

In a further study of a small number of cohesive ties (Chapman 1981) used a modified cloze procedure to detect developmental trends in the perception of cohesion. In this he contrasted the ability of 6 and 7 year olds with that of 9 and 10 year olds to replace the deletions. The results supported the predictions in that as well as significant increases in the number of verbatim responses (i.e. replacement of the word the author used), there were clear indications of the use of cohesive words that were not the deleted word.

Following these studies, a longitudinal research programme led by Chapman began to yield preliminary results. (This programme will be discussed more fully in the next chapter.) An indication of the results was given at a UKRA conference in 1982. Using the data collected in Cambridgeshire schools the ability of 8, 10 and 13-year-old children to perceive cohesive elements in their reading texts was reported. These results (Chapman 1983a) as well as showing variations in the perception of particular types of tie, confirmed the developmental trends found earlier.

Irwin (1980) manipulated the number of cohesive ties in reading passages so that there were many more in some than in the others. She found that the number and types of cohesive ties affected the later recall of the passages.

Nunan (1983a) designed a study to test the efficiency of cloze procedure as a measure of meaning relationships beyond the sentence. These were classified into 'S' deletions, those having significance within the sentence and 'T' deletions, whose significance lay beyond the boundary of the sentence. Using post-graduate students as his readers Nunan gave them passages that conformed to the meaning relationships in question. To another group he gave the same passage with the sentences randomized. His results suggest that deletions probing semantic relationships which go beyond the sentence boundaries make cloze and effective instrument for measuring intersentential comprehension.

In a further study, Nunan (1983b) working with cohesive ties, tried to ascertain whether the distance between the presupposed and the presupposing items in a cohesive tie was a significant factor in the ability of secondary level readers. His subjects were in year nine of an Australian High School and were judged by their teachers to be of average ability. Five of the subjects were second language speakers of English and the rest were native speakers.

Two passages were selected for the study such that the writer's style would be general, be long enough for 64 cloze type deletions, be within the reading ability of the subjects and be typical of school texts. The test situation conformed as closely to the normal school situation as possible.

The passages were analysed for both inter- (T) and intra- (S) sentential cohesion and were matched so that there were equal numbers of 'T' and 'S' deletions. The findings were that the students found the 'S' deletions significantly easier to replace, that is, when both ends of the cohesive tie were within the same sentence, than the 'T' deletions which called for integration across the sentence boundary.

It was concluded that it is not the cohesive device itself that causes difficulty. Nunan suggests that the distance across which readers must integrate information in the 'T' situation makes demands on short term memory capacity and may downgrade skills already acquired.

Hadley (1985) investigated the relationship between the perception of anaphoric personal reference items and reading comprehension. Her subjects, who were drawn from three different year levels in a primary school, were tested on their ability to comprehend certain anaphoric items. She used two methods to achieve her results, one sought the resolution of the antecedents of the anaphoric items and the second required the replacement of words or phrases with the correct anaphoric items. She found that certain items were recognized more easily than others, but that items embedded in direct speech caused most difficulty. A steady development was found in the perception of anaphoric items as children moved through school levels. Girls were superior to boys in the early and middle years of the primary school, but no difference was found in the upper level of the school. The findings pointed to a significant relationship between the perception of the selected anaphoric personal reference items and general reading proficiency as measured by standardized reading tests.

Smith and Elkins (1985), working with a sample of sixth grade male poor readers, compared the miscues they made on cohesive items when reading two expository passages with miscues in general. The subjects were also asked to recall the passages. The main findings of their study indicated that there were no differences in performance between the two passages but that the subjects lost meaning and syntax more frequently on cohesive items, and that their inability to use cohesion adversely affected recall of the passages.

The research of Smith and Elkins is interesting as it emphasizes semantic and contextual aspects of cohesion. In particular they draw attention to componential and organic cohesion analysis as proposed by Halliday and Hasan (1980) and Hasan (1984). In this development of cohesion analysis, componential cohesion on the one hand is said to create relationships in three ways, by co-reference, co-classification and co-extension. Organic cohesion on the other hand is cohesion achieved by connectives and repetition of theme (see also Smith and Elkins 1984).

These studies are reported more fully in Smith (1985). In this thesis she stresses the importance of the semantic aspects of cohesion, suggesting that other studies had not done so. She concludes that 'cohesion in text is an important factor to be considered in evaluating the structure of text and in reading theory and practice'.

Worall (1985) deomonstrated how a reader's use of cohesive ties can be examined as part of miscue analysis. Her subjects were grade three children of high, average and low ability. She found that readers who were proficient produced miscues that did not change meaning or corrected their miscues so that meaning was not disturbed. Poor readers tended not to correct their miscues, but when they did they tended to retain meaning.

Steffenson (1981) investigated the relationship of register and cohesion in text comprehension in three cross-cultural studies. Using the insights on prior knowledge from schema theory, she found that her predictions that 'the ways in which subjects used the linguistic reflexes that indicate the situation of the speech event and those that create textual cohesion would be affected by their cultural knowledge, assumptions and beliefs', were supported.

Binkley (1983) examined cohesive ties within the writings of various disciplines to discover whether their patternings differed. She collected 10 sample paragraphs from 10 graduate and undergraduate textbooks from five disciplines: physics, biology, economics, political science and history. She carried out a frequency count for each sample and grouped them in two ways, according to structural class and by functional category so as to determine whether the distribution of ties was influenced by subject discipline.

Her findings showed that when the frequency of the ties is grouped by structural category, there is homogeneity within each field. When frequency is grouped by function, there is homogeneity within biology and physics, with the other disciplines showing greater variability. In addition, there were significant differences in the distribution of ties such as could be attributed to the influence of academic disciplines.

Writers in the disciplines of physics and biology were found to rely heavily on 'the' and the repetition of lexical items, giving a high degree of clarity and formality to the texts. Economics and political science used pronominals more frequently than demonstratives whilst there was a more even distribution between repetition of the same lexical item and synonym. History was found to use collocation, synonyms and repetition of the same lexical item indicating a greater dependence on the prior vocabulary knowledge of the readers.

Bridge and Winograde (1982) investigated the ability of ninth grade good and poor readers to complete a cloze passage in which three kinds of cohesive relationships (referential, conjunctive and lexical) had been systematically deleted. The subjects were asked to read the passage orally, supply the missing words and to think aloud about their responses. The results of the study showed that the subjects were aware of cohesive relationships and generally used them to supply the missing words. Interestingly, the subjects varied their use of intrasentential and intersentential information based upon the type of cohesion involved.

Phillips and Zinan (reported in Chapman 1981) made a study of readability and cohesion factors in a basal reading scheme for children between the ages of 6 and 12 years. They point out that the series had a controlled vocabulary and that the vocabulary development is usually accompanied by an increase in sentence length. The series contained both expository and narrative prose.

They found that certain cohesive ties predominated at certain levels. In the primer, for example, although personal reference ties are the most frequent, conjunction ties also appear. Interestingly, although the simple conjunctions such as 'and' and 'but' appear throughout the series, they usually occur at the beginning of sentences in the early books; then, as the sentences become more complex, they are incorporated within the sentence. Referring to lexical cohesion, reiteration and collocation, they suggest that in the early readers, reiteration probably reflects the lack of other cohesive elements. They also point out that lexical cohesion through collocation, or association of related words, can also be found in the primer helping to carry the theme of each story.

Using the concept of texture in teaching English as a foreign language, Williams (1983) outlined the system of cohesive relations, described problematic instances in the recognition of cohesive ties, and suggested appropriate teaching materials and classroom techniques. In doing this he suggests that the materials and procedures outlined have relevance in teaching the recognition of cohesive ties in any foreign language.

Working with teachers of pupils from minority ethnic groups, Wishart (1987) developed a teaching strategy to help the pupils attend to the cohesive elements in texts alongside the conceptual content. She reports that 'the teachers found that they developed their own awareness of the linguistic demands on pupils of the texts which they selected, and the response of the pupils demonstrated the contribution of the cohesive elements of the texts to the interplay of the factors, linguistic and conceptual, which influence pupils 'effective reading'.

Cohesion research related to writing

One of the first studies using cohesion analysis is that of Pettegrew (1981) who compared the language development of 6 and 7 year old children. The children provided oral texts in two narrative contexts, retelling a story that had been read to them, and dictating an original story to an adult scribe. The children were categorized at three levels of literacy development (fluent readers, transitional readers and beginning readers). Six groups of cohesive relations were used, reference, substitutions, ellipsis, conjunctions, lexical cohesion and exophoric reference. Pettegrew found that patterns of texture for the three literacy groups were significantly different. Discrimination among the groups of children was greatest between the fluent and the beginning readers, with the transitional readers falling between the two extreme groups. The differences were attributable to the relative use of exophoric reference and lexical cohesion. The use of exophoric presupposition coupled with a regular increase across groups in the use of lexical cohesion was observed as literacy developed.

The results suggested a shift, with literacy acquisition, the greater textual explicitness marking a growing ability to use language in direct and abstract contexts of situations. No sex differences were reported in the patterns of texture, but there were differences in the two narrative tasks with the children showing greater control in the dictation task. No evidence of differences in syntactic development were found.

Rutter and Raban (1982) examined the development of the use of cohesive ties in the free writing of children aged 6 to 10 years. They found that the pre-eminent category of tie used was reference and this was followed by lexical cohesion. The other three categories (substitution, ellipsis and conjunction) were found only infrequently with substitution rarely appearing. Little difference was found in the proportion of cohesive ties to all words written as a function of age or sex. Though more cohesive ties were used by the other children, they formed a lower proportion of their total output. The differences between boys and girls within each age group was reported to be marked. Six-year-old boys used ellipsis with greater frequency than girls while the girls at 10 used ellipsis more than boys. The girls use more conjunctions and lexical cohesion as opposed to the boy's greater proportional use of reference and substitution. Finally, the range and variety of cohesive devices employed by 10-year-old children was reported to differ substantially from those used by the 6 year olds.

Yde and Spoelders (1985) investigated the text-productive ability of Dutch-speaking children, including 'the devices for cohesion and compactness'. Writing samples from 8 and 9 year olds, and 10 and 11 year olds in narrative texts were compared and 'a developmental trend in the construction of more cohesive and compact narrative texts' was found.

In a study of the relationship between text coherence, cohesion and writing quality, McCulley (1983) analysed a sample of 493 papers from the 2,794 persuasive papers written by 17 year olds during the 1978–79 national writing assessment by the National Assessment of Educational Progress in the United States of America. He reports that 'coherence, but not cohesion is a valid construct of judged writing quality; although the evidence is not so strong when manuscript length is held constant'. Taking this into account, he states that 'textual' cohesion might be a far more important attribute of coherence than it is presently considered'.

Summary of cohesion research related to reading

Evidence from these indicate that:

- the ability to perceive and process cohesive ties is associated with reading proficiency and comprehending. Chapman (1979a, 1979b, 1983), Nunan (1983b), Hadley (1985) and Smith (1985).
- the perception of cohesive ties is subject to a developmental pattern. Chapman and Stokes (1980), Chapman (1981, 1983a and 1983b), Anderson (1983a), Hadley (1985), Moberly (1978).
- the pattern of development is related to cohesive tie types so that the order in the early years from easy to difficult is: reference, lexical cohesion, substitution/ellipsis, conjunction. Moberly (1978) and Monson (n.d.).
- the number and types of cohesive ties affect text recall. Irwin (1980) and Smith (1985).
- of the distance factors, immediate, mediated and remote, it is the remote inter-sentential or textual ties that are significantly difficult to process. Moberly (1978), Nunan (1983a).
- anaphoric reference embedded in direct speech is more difficult to recognize than it is in other forms. Hadley (1985).
- there are sex differences in the ability of children to handle cohesive ties efficiently. Moberly (1978).
- there are indications of differential effects according to the register of the text. Binkley (1983).
- the relationship of cohesion and register to text comprehension is affected by cultural knowledge, assumptions and beliefs. Steffenson (1981).
- cohesive tie perception as an addition to miscue analysis has diagnostic possibilities. Worrall (1985), Smith and Elkins (1984).
- very different methods have been used to uncover the above effects and relationships; a modified cloze procedure has been particularly efficient in this respect. Moberly (1978), Nunan (1983b), Chapman (1979c, 1981, 1983b), Smith (1985), Bridge and Winograde (1982), Irwin (1980), Anderson E. (1983), Hadley (1985), Worall (1985), Steffenson (1986).

Criticisms of cohesion research

Most of the foregoing studies have had positive results, but as with all research that is breaking new ground, cohesion research has had its critics. And we now relate some of the problems that have been raised.

Perhaps the most influential, theoretically, has been the critique made by Morgan and Sellner (1980) of discourse and linguistic theory. One of the theories they criticized was that of Halliday and Hasan (1976), that is their proposals for cohesion. In their critique they state that the main issue in the discourse theories they discuss is quite simple:

> It is this: How much of the competence that underlies the ability to understand and construct discourse is specifically linguistic, and how much is just the

manifestation, in use in language, of mental systems more general than linguistic competence.

They go on to point out that a clear conception of linguistic theory is needed to answer this question. They clearly favour Chomsky's linguistics, although they do not acknowledge this, in that they state the goal of linguistics to be:

> Constructing a theory that treats those parts of human knowledge that are involved only in knowledge of language (and its acquisition), rather than being instances of more general cognitive abilities.

When this theoretical stance is applied to cohesion it leads them to question some of Halliday and Hasan's statements. For example, the description of anaphoric reference to which we alluded at the beginning of this chapter, is challenged. The actual quote is from a cookery book:

> Wash and core six cooking apples. Put them into a fireproof dish.
> (Halliday and Hasan 1976:2)

Halliday and Hasan use the anaphoric relationship between 'them' and 'six cooking apples' as an illustration, pointing out that 'cohesion is affected not only by the presence of the referring item alone but by the presence of both the referring item and the item it refers to'.

Morgan and Sellner challenge this stating that 'them' does not refer back to something that has gone before. 'It refers', they claim, '(more accurately the writer *uses* it to refer) to six cooking apples, not the noun phrase *six cooking apples*. The sentence is an instruction to put apples, not words, into a dish'.

This is only a small part of this criticism but we hope it is enough to give you an idea of the kind of discussion that is entailed.

Our comment is that language is first and foremost a symbol system and when we use words, we use them symbolically in place of objects. Few would misunderstand the meaning intended by Halliday and Hasan in their use of 'refer back'. And here there may be a misunderstanding in that linguists, when analysing a written text treat it as inert and look at the location of the antecendent (six cooking apples) on the page in relation to the anaphor (them). In this they understand the anaphor to refer back. What is of greater interest here however, is the notion of directionality in procesing. In this case the presupposing nature of cohesion does not involve literal referral back when reading. Rather, the reader, on meeting a name or theme of a sentence anticipates the anaphor in a forward acting manner. That is, on reading the pronoun, 'them' there is no mental looking back for the antecedent, 'six cooking apples'. The knowledge of the topic is carried forward and the reader understands that when the author uses the word 'them' his meaning is clear, but this does not invalidate the description given by Halliday and Hasan.

A more important criticism of Morgan and Sellner's account is the attempt to separate the linguistic from the cognitive aspects of discourse. This probably harks back to the Piagetian stance that cognitive and linguistic features have separate beginnings in the child's development. As we will go on to show there is little to be gained theoretically and certainly not in practice by this separation. It is more constructive to accept the position of Vygotsky (1962) who instances word meaning as an exemplar of the psychological and linguistic:

> The meaning of a word represents such a close amalgam of thought and language that it is hard to tell whether it is a phenomenon of thought. A word without meaning is an empty sound; meaning therefore, is a criterion of 'word', its indispensable component.
>
> (Vygotsky 1962:120)

Or just as pertinently:

> Thought is not merely expressed in words; it comes into existence through them.
>
> (Vygotsky 1962:125)

If we adopt the position that cohesion involves both cognitive and linguistic factors, we will find that the approach of Halliday and Hasan stands up well to the criticisms. In making this point we are not saying that Halliday and Hasan involve psychological aspects in their work although they do not deny them.

There is, of course, a great deal more to be said on this topic, but we will leave it until Chapter 8 and to other volumes.

CHAPTER 4

Reading research in the UK

Much of the research mentioned in the previous chapter was concerned with our increasing knowledge of the reading process. We report in this chapter, however, research that moves into the school to gather data primarily about the teaching and progress of reading development. Obviously, the work will not be devoid of concern with developments in thinking about reading but the work does concentrate on application. We summarize two major investigation first, and then go on to report on the cohesion research carried out at the Open University in more detail.

1. Research at Nottingham University

In their Schools Council project, Lunzer and Gardner (1979) carried out investigations in three areas concerned with reading and its teaching. These were:

1. on the nature of comprehension.
2. a description of classroom practice related to reading.
3. an evaluation of methods of improving reading to learn.

Two important findings came out of the research into comprehension; the first was that reading was found to be a single aptitude that cannot be broken down into sub-skills. They also found no support for the notion that some children might 'possess' lower-order skills, like letter and word recognition, but not higher-order skills, like comprehension.

Their contribution in respect to comprehension was to re-introduce the concept of reflection, in that they propose that individual differences in the willingness and ability of children to reflect on what is being read. They suggest a broad framework to foster understanding. These include:

1. reading situations designed to foster a willingness to reflect on what is being read.
2. a structure of instruction, guidance and reading practice which improves the quality of instruction.

3. a perusal of methods and materials aimed at creating the optimum opportunity for pupils to use reading purposefully.

(Lunzer and Gardner 1979:301)

When observing classroom activities they found a considerable difference in lesson patterns in final-year primary and first-year secondary school classes. These differences were signalled by:

1. a decrease in individual tuition and an increase in 'teacher informing' at first-year secondary level.
2. a significant increase in pupil time spent 'listening' at first-year secondary level.
3. a marked increase in the use of text-books in all subjects except mathematics at first-year secondary level.

(ibid:302)

As a result of their studies they also note:

> It seems possible, therefore, that whereas the less able reader becomes increasingly conscious of his disability, the average and above-average reader finds less use for his reading and relegates it to an inferior position. A 'reading' homework becomes a soft option not a challenge.

(ibid:303)

More than 50% of the reading across all subjects in secondary school was done in short bursts of 1 to 15 seconds, mitigating against the development of reading of continuous texts.

The project team went on to recommend ways of investigating texts and these useful procedures will be referred to later in this and the other volumes in the series.

2. Research at Manchester University

This Schools Council project was carried out by Southgate and her colleagues and was based at the University of Manchester. It was essentially a fact-finding investigation which studied the progress of children, who had achieved average reading standards, for two years.

The report of the project (Southgate *et al.* 1981) contains a useful summary of devlopments in our knowledge of reading to that time. They state that 'current attempts to define reading tend to regard it as a thinking process, with attention focussed on comprehension'. They also note the direction of recent research regarding background knowledge during comprehension, in that the reader contributes from his or her own knowledge when comprehending. They record the view emphasized by Lunzer and Gardner that comprehension is a 'global act' and not a collection of sub-skills. However, they do not dismiss traditional methods of the teaching of reading.

During the project teachers were asked for their practical needs and in this they expressed two areas of concern. Firstly, they required more knowledge of the particular stage of reading development under scrutiny. Secondly, they wanted more information about assessment, diagnosis and record keeping. However, 'only a small minority appreciated the need to ensure that a firm basis for both functional and recreational reading be laid down during the first two years of the junior school.'

The summary findings of the project state that many children aged 7 to 9 years were learning to read effectively; however, there were certain children of average reading ability who did not make the progress anticipated.

The major recommendations of the project suggest four modifications to present practice.

1. A drastic curtailment is needed of teacher's almost universal practice of spending the major portion of their time in reading periods in attempting to listen to large numbers of individual children reading to them for extremely brief periods each, from teacher-selected reading books.
2. An increase in the length of time which teachers spend with individual children is recommended, but with such contacts occurring at less frequent intervals.
3. The provision of periods in which every child in the class is silently reading, without interruption, books of his own choice, should be extended. The length of such periods should be progressively increased as the children grow accustomed to them.
4. Experimental plans for radically reducing the lengthy amounts of time in which teachers are acting solely as consultants for individual children on the correct spelling of words, should be made and put into practice as a matter of urgency.

3. Research at the Open University

The Open University reading survey

The reasons for setting up this project, which was considered to be breaking new ground, were threefold. First, the findings of the research team at Nottingham University, particularly those regarding the problems associated with the transfer from primary to secondary school, created uncertainty about reading progress in schools. Secondly, during the construction of an Open University course for the inservice education of teachers, PE232 Language Development, it was found that there was insufficient knowledge about reading development to properly advise teachers. Thirdly, previous research (Chapman, 1970) had shown the inappropriateness of some linguistic research paradigms as a basis for planning the teaching of reading.

As the results of this project have not been completely reported elsewhere, we give an account here of the philosophy and methodology of the project and a summary of results in this and the next chapter. As the work was extensive, some of the results will be given in other volumes in this series. The information gained from this work also forms the basis of the exploration into the teaching of reading that follows in the later chapters.

The aims of the research, which was supported for a time by the Department of Education and Science, were:

1. To identify, validate and establish the educational significance of some recently described textlinguistic features.
2. To trace by a longitudinal reading research programme, children's mastery of the linguistic features selected from the data provided in 1) above.
3. To contribute to the theoretical debate on reading and textlinguistics from the data collected in 2) above.

The thinking that resulted from the first of these aims has already been discussed in Chapter 2 where the language description provided by Halliday and his colleagues was selected as being the most practically useful and theoretically informative for the teaching of language in schools. This was for many reasons but primarily because it (a) provides a *functional* account of language, and (b) deals with language as *discourse* (beyond the level of the sentence). All this makes it attractive from the practical, teaching point of view. There is no other account that so comprehensively covers the main aspects of language needed by teachers in primary and secondary schools.

To achieve the second aim, that is to glean information about reading development in terms of the linguistic features selected, it is necessary to observe many children of different ages reading the texts they use day by day in the classroom. It is also preferable for these observations to be made longitudinally. That is, the type of data required needs to be collected from the same children as they go through the school system. This has the undoubted advantage of releasing the analyses of data from many statistical restraints. It was beyond the resources available, however, to pursue the ideal plan of following children's progress throughout their complete schooling, but it was possible to select three groups of children aged 8, 10 and 13 years and to follow each of these groups for a three-year period. The number of children needed was large and arrangements were made with two Local Education Authorities, one urban and one mostly rural, to work with some 1,500 children. There were twice as many children in the urban schools as in the rural area. There were few children in the sample for whom remedial reading had been prescribed or children whose mother tongue was other than English. As in the Manchester project, the children consisted largely of those making at least average progress in reading, with the majority being beyond the initial stages of learning to read.

At the beginning of the survey the children were allocated by class groupings into three Cohorts. The second year junior children (8 years) comprised Cohort A, the fourth year junior children (10 years) Cohort B and the second year secondary children (13 years) Cohort C.

At the conclusion of the first data collection of the number of children having completed all the tasks were Cohort A, 436, Cohort B, 474 and Cohort C, 445, that is 1,355 in all. The children were drawn from 23 schools in the first year of the project. These large groups were necessary to give a spread of ability and to meet the decline in numbers anticipated during the three years due to movement, illness and other causes.

By the time the third year of the project was reached, there were 392 (-44) in

Cohort A, 362 (-112) in Cohort B and 378 (-67) in Cohort C for whom we had complete records. You will notice that the greatest loss was in the years covering the transfer from primary to secondary school. This was largely because some of the children were dispersed so thinly that it was uneconomical to try to find them in the many schools to which they had transferred. Nonetheless, the number for whom the project had total records was more than sufficient to support the credibility of the research findings.

Philosophy and rationale

It was deemed most important for the study to have *ecological validity*. This concept (see Bronfenbrenner, 1976) involves designing educational research so that its findings can be directly translated into classroom practice. This is most important not only on theoretical grounds but so that teachers would give its findings credence. It also seemed to us essential that, as this was a study of reading meant to have direct relevance to the teaching of reading, that the reading materials used in the study should be based on the materials normally used in schools with children of these particular age-groups. There are, as we saw above in the Nottingham research, good reasons to suppose that it is the texts themselves that pose some of the problems for readers (Harrison, 1979). It is often the case that materials on which the children are tested are written specially to control such variables as word frequency, syntactic structure or other linguistic features. This is done because the focus of the research is linguistic and only marginally educational. Such procedures would, it is suggested, provide the research with a false basis from the start. There would be no guarantee that the results of such simulation would transfer to the real world and may well give a false impression as to how reading was actually developing. It was decided therefore, to work with texts obtained from schools and collect data in as near as normal classroom situations as could be arranged.

It is not difficult to put together a representative collection of texts from across the subjects in a modern curriculum for different age levels. It is much more difficult to design a method to find out whether those texts are being comprehended as they are being read. As the reading process is not directly observable, methods have to be employed that will enable the researcher to infer what is happening inside children's heads.

The second major methodological problem then was to obtain data of the covert process of silent reading itself. To do this, it is necessary in the first place to require the reader to make a response of some kind so that observations can be made. The cognitive processes involved in reading are unseen (or unseeable) and all such observations, no matter the method, will necessitate that inferences be made by the researcher as to what is happening. In reading, particularly reading passages of some length silently, it is impossible to enter the process directly without stopping and thereby altering the process. For reading is essentially dynamic and to stop it prematurely only halts the processes involved without necessarily illuminating them. This is particularly crucial when the factors of cohesion and register, which are to do with recovering the unity of the text, are concerned. Furthermore, to adopt the traditional practice of waiting until the text has been read in its entirety and then to ask questions as in the traditional comprehension test, not only calls for the inferences already referred to but has additional complications, such as those related to the reader's prior, or background, knowledge for that particular content information. In addition, the types of comprehension question asked to infer the reader's understanding may also prove an additional complication. Comprehension assessed by questions has been bedevilled by problems of this kind as so clearly identified in the work of Tuinman in the early seventies. Tuinman (1973/1974) selected five comprehension tests and separated the questions asked from the passages to which they related. Some of the children worked the complete test and others answered the questions only. It was found that correct responses without the passages were well above what was expected. That is many questions could be answered from prior or background knowledge without reference to the passage. In this you might like to compare the comprehension questions on 'Whales' designed by the team at the Assessment and Performance Unit (DES 1981). You might like to estimate how many children might well know the answers without needing to pay much attention to the text on which they are based. And finally, and most importantly, testing reading in this way, that is by questioning, tells us very little about the process of reading (Chapman, 1983a). It was decided therefore, that a new methodology was needed; such a methodology would employ, among other things, the concepts of cohesion and register to uncover the extent of the underlying and developing textlinguistic knowledge (that is, the combined knowledge of texts and language) of children in the age range 8 to 15 years.

The starting point for thinking about the methodology needed was Goodman's miscue analysis (Goodman 1973) to which we have already referred. This is one of the most interesting methods to date for observing the reading process in the school situation. Furthermore, it is a method which avoids many of the problems mentioned above. In this procedure the reader reads aloud passages which are difficult enough to generate a sufficient number of errors or, as Goodman prefers to call them, miscues. These errors are then analysed for their probable origins according to a three-layered cueing system, graphophonic, syntactic and semantic. This gives the observer considerable information regarding the strength or otherwise of the reader's underlying textlinguistic base. Using this technique it becomes possible to examine a child's reading performance without upsetting its dynamic quality. As Goodman puts it, it provides the researcher or teacher with a 'window on the reading process'. Although still requiring inferences to be drawn this method has given new insights (Gollasch 1982). However, there were considerable limitations which made its use highly problematic for our own research.

In the first place miscue analysis requires the reader to read the passages selected aloud and this in itself involves different processes from those involved in silent reading. Next, and in some ways more perplexing, children not experiencing difficulty with their reading as required to read materials that are beyond their present level of reading development so as to create sufficient errors for analysis. It is suggested that if this is so, then the results may be suspect for it is unlikely that they will be true representation of that child's normal reading (Anderson 1981). Further, as it has to be applied individually, its time-consuming nature will inhibit the number of children and texts needing to be examined. For the purposes of a longitudinal project with large numbers of children and requiring the investigation of many texts, the cost would be prohibitive as many trained observers would be needed over long periods of time. What was required by this project, therefore, was a method that allowed many texts of some length to be read silently by many children in normal classroom conditions yet retaining the ability to detect textlinguistic growth.

To meet these demands a new type of error analysis procedure was evolved, which we believe preserves the notion of a 'window on the reading process' but allows group presentation. Instead of, as it were, creating problems in the child by presenting too difficult texts, the new procedure asks the child to read the same texts that have been selected by their teachers as being suitable for day to day use but that have been 'adjusted'. This adjustment was done by removing one end of a cohesive tie from the text so as to create a gap, the presence of which was indicated by double lines of standard length (see illustration on page 62). The cohesive ties chosen for this were considered to be part of a prominent chain of ties that ran through the text. The reader was then asked to fill in the gap with an appropriate word. (In doing this, the method resembles a modified or rational cloze procedure, but due to important differences is called GAP to avoid misinterpretation and comparisons with traditional cloze.)

The rationale of the procedure depends upon the presupposition factor of the cohesive tie mentioned earlier, that is, the identification of some item (the deleted) being dependent on another (usually earlier in the text) for its full interpretation. Very few deletions were made so as to interrupt the story or meaning of the text as little as possible. Typically, three or four deletions per page of text to be read were made. If the child replaced the author's word successfully, then it was deemed that the cohesion existing between the clauses had been perceived. It was also found on later examination that many words, other than the author's word, that satisfied the cohesive requirements were given by the children. These were also analysed in detail and became one of the main features of the research. The cohesive ties were sampled according to the categories and sub-categories of reference, substitution, conjunction and lexical cohesion listed in Chapter 2. It should be noted that ellipsis could not be sampled by this method. However, in the qualitative analysis performed on the data, there were clear signs of its effect. We will be looking at the type of analysis in this and the following chapter.

A collection of classroom books were made (a) from amongst those often chosen by children as their library book choice, (b) from among the books most often read to children by their teachers, and (c) books most often purchased by schools as non-fictional material, i.e. information books for the junior children and text books for the secondary children. (Lists of the books selected appear in Appendix 1.)

About 100 books were collected and from these a further selection was made so that extracts of some length could be used for the purpose of identifying chains of cohesive ties. These were then further divided into two groups to accord with the two major registers divisions, fiction and non-fiction. This procedure yielded 61 excerpts which were put, after pilot testing, into four booklets, two for the junior group in Cohort A and two for the older children in Cohorts B and C. It is important to note here that the original intention was to have two booklets for each cohort but it was discovered during pilot testing that sufficient responses were not forthcoming from the children in Cohort C on the materials that were used in their classrooms to make a feasible analysis. Some of the texts from this age group were discarded therefore and the rest incorporated in the materials originally designed for Cohort B.

The booklets containing the Gap deletions in cohesive chains were: Junior Booklet 1 (fiction) containing extracts from 14 books, Junior Booklet 2 (non-fiction) from 19 books. Secondary Booklet 3 (fiction) from 13 books and Secondary Booklet 4 (non-fiction) from 16 books. The length of the passages varied from instances of short paragraphs as in mathematical textbooks to two or three pages of continuous texts. There were 60 deletions of cohesive ties in each booklet making a total of 130 for each set. Five other deletions of words, not considered to be inter-sentential in character, were made to contrast with the cohesive deletions and to check the procedures. These are called 'other' deletions in the analyses that follow.

Alongside these specially prepared booklets, standardized test of reading (NFER Reading Test AD, and NFER Reading Test EH1 and Ravens Matrices) were also administered for comparing the verbal and non-verbal abilities of the project children with standardized samples and for checking the consistency of the cohorts as children moved from school to school.

It should be emphasized that these methodological decisions were reached after a number of pilot tests. During this early phase multiple choice testing was rejected because of extensive problems of providing distractors.

In-depth studies

Alongside the reading survey, a series of in-depth, or converging, studies were carried out into areas arising from our own and the research of others. As we have seen in the previous chapters, this was a time of lively enquiry into the reading process, and some of this on-going research had a bearing on the direction we were following.

In addition, it was felt wise to be cautious as we were well aware of breaking new ground and of the limitations of any research methodology for there is no perfect method of gathering this type of data. Furthermore, as a decision had been made to ensure that the findings are ecologically valid. This did not relieve us of the responsibility to work in a sufficiently rigorous way for the findings to have validity.

It was decided, therefore, to mount a series of in-depth studies alongside the survey data to resolve a number of issues. These studies were created and carried out mainly by Eleanor Anderson for the research team.

A number of studies of factors arising from the methodology of the survey needed to be tested out, particularly the part played by cohesion during reading. Indeed, one of the main thrusts of the research concerned this very issue. However, it is important to point out the research's main function was not conceived as an attempt to verify the concept of cohesion per se, for that would be a task for linguists and would be beyond the scope of the project. Rather the main task given was to investigate the part played by cohesion and register in reading in such a way as to provide guidance to teachers in their day to day classroom practice. In research teams, it was applied research. This fact must be emphasized, for the initial funding and direction came from Schools Branch of the DES, and was made perfectly clear to us at the first meeting of the project's Steering Committee. It is also one of the reasons why the research is being reported for the first time here, in a book which attempts to relate the research findings directly to the work of teachers and schools.

Study 1. Extending the context

The strength of cloze procedure is that it enable the reader to draw on all the available context to replace the deletion. As there are a number of factors involved, one of the problems raised by this methodology was to be reasonably sure that the completion of a cohesive gap really did require, to a significant degree, the perception of cohesion.

It was clear in the first place that there would be a heavy loading on the cohesion factor, for unlike random deletions in traditional cloze, a central feature of this method was the removal of one end, the presupposed, of a cohesive tie from a cohesive chain . It was argued that the ability to perceive the cohesion of the text at that point would be strongly involved in the closure of such a gap. But was that involvement a significant factor? This was the question the first in-depth study attempted to answer.

Our first thoughts on this were to propose that if there were cohesive elements then there might well be non-cohesive elements. If it could be shown that the processing of cohesive and non-cohesive elements were significantly different, then we would have gone a long way to solving the issue. However, this position is theoretically unsound, for there is no such thing in authentic texts as a non-cohesive element. There are two different types of cohesion, one within the sentence (intra-sentential), and one occuring across sentence boundaries (inter-sentential). It is the latter that has been recognized as the important factor in the development of reading, although the former cannot be discounted. The telling factor in this is that intra-sentential cohesion involves a different level of processing than inter-sentential cohesion. This arises from the theoretical reasons outlined above and later again in Chapter 5. The problem was largely resolved by a study which investigated three levels of processing, that involved in completing a deletion in a single isolated sentence (I version), the processing involved in completing a deletion of one end of a cohesive tie with the other end present (T version), and the processing involved in completing the deletion in the full text (C version).

The 96 children chosen to take part in this study came from a school in a different Local Education Authority from those in the survey. The children, who were in their fourth year at secondary school (15 year olds), cooperated readily once the purpose of the work was explained to them.

The materials used were drawn from the survey booklets such that:

1. in the booklet presenting the isolated sentences, version (I), there were 69 single sentences, one per page, with one deletion in each sentence;
2. the Tied (T) version booklets contained 69 pairs of sentences with a deletion in one sentence and the other end of the cohesive tie in the proceeding sentence.
3. The Context version (C) booklets contained the 15 complete passages from which the (I) and (T) versions were taken.

An illustration of these three contexts appears in Figure 6.

On the first testing occasion five classes of 15-year-old students attempted the isolated sentence version for the first time (I1) and a standardized reading test (NFER EH1). On the next occasion, approximately a third of the group attempted the (I) version again (I2) a third attempted the (T) version and the other third, the (C) version.

The children were divided into 26 sets of three subjects per set where they were closely matched in reading score. The difference scores were then found by subtracting the (I1) score from the score obtained on the second occasion.

The (T) and (C) versions had significantly higher scores than the (I2) condition, (p>0.01), but did not differ significantly from each other. Although there was an increase in score between (I1) and (I2) this was not significant.

A large number of cohesive ties and tie types were investigated: 17 reference types, 15 substitutions, 21 conjuctions and 11 lexical items.

A further 5 items, which were intra-cohesive and termed 'other', were also examined but the difference between performance on the first and second occasion was not significant. (For histograms of these results see Chapman and Anderson 1982.)

It was quite clear from this study that when one end of a cohesive tie is removed children's ability to restore it relies mainly on three sources of

Example from Isolated Version Booklet

When _____ came, they found themselves possessed of a great deal of knowledge concerning gas turbine engines.

Example from Tied Version Booklet

During the war they worked with Whittle on his aero engines. When _____ came, they found themselves possessed of a great deal of knowledge concerning gas turbine engines.

Example from Context Version Booklet

Turbine-powered cars

In the war, too, were laid the seeds of another great chapter in the story of motoring. Frank Whittle's work on jet engines for aeroplanes was later to lead to the development of the world's first turbine cars. ════════ it was the Rover company who played a big part in this too.

During the war, they worked with Whittle on his aero engines. When ════════ came, they found themselves possessed of a great deal of knowledge concerning gas turbine engines. ════════ they were in the car business not the aircraft industry.

Rovers set out to find if the gas turbine could be adapted to a motor-car. It could and it was and in 1952, the Rover JET 1 set up the first officially recognized international speed records for turbine-powered cars. ══════════════ a Rover-BRM sports-racing car powered with a turbine unit has run very successfully at Le Mans and Chrysler, in America, have produced a remarkably impressive passenger saloon car using the same means of propulsion.

Figure 6

information. One of these is the register of the text and this factor will be analysed by the qualitive analysis later. The other two sources are structural (from within the sentence) and the inter-sentential cohesion present in that part of the text. The extent to which these two have been separated in the study allows an estimate of the contribution of each. Although there are variations according to cohesive tie types, the results demonstrate that a significant proportion of the gain in scores comes from the presence of the cohesive tie relationship when the text extends beyond the sentence. This is particularly so when the gain scores on the 'other' items are examined, for these show very little increase in score indeed. In summary then, inter-sentential cohesion was the most significant factor in replacing the deletion.

These results were interpreted as giving considerable support to the validity of the test of the perception of the cohesion being used in the survey. The results were also supported by the work of Nunan (1983b) which we reviewed in Chapter 3.

The study also answered two other important but subsidiary questions, these were to seek for practice effects and to find if there was a ceiling effect in the tests. There was no ceiling effect with these 15 year olds and the practice effect was negligible considering the closeness in time the tests were given. It was decided that the practice effect that might occur if the survey test were given on three annual occasions could be discounted.

Some linguists have expressed concern over the imprecision of cloze; however, this study showed that, for our purposes, the selective cloze methodology was measuring inter-sentential cohesion. However, we needed to delve further into the relationship of cohesion with other text factors.

Study 2. Prior knowledge, levels of cohesion and comprehension

In the review of research we noted that a contribution was made by the reader's prior-knowledge to the understanding of a passage. Other research (Irwin 1980) had suggested that the level of explicit cohesion, that is whether there were more or less cohesive ties in one passage, might also influence comprehension. It was decided therefore to mount a study to investigate possible relationships between these factors in reading comprehension.

It was hypothesized that there would be high scores on comprehension tests where the reader has considerable prior knowledge on a topic and where there is a high level of explicit cohesion in the text being comprehended.

In order to test this, 16 passages on two topics, eight on 'heat' and eight on 'conservation' were especially prepared. There was one high cohesion version and one low cohesion version on each of the eight subjects. There were at least twice as many cohesive ties in the high level version as the low level version. The number of words and sentences was kept constant across the two versions.

Each passages was followed by 11 multiple choice questions as proposed by Anderson (1976: 106):

> 2 on vocabulary.
> 2 on details in the text.
> 2 on sequences in the text.
> 2 on causal relations in the text.
> 1 containing the main idea of the passage.
> 2 on inference from the text.

The sample comprised four classes of 9 and 10-year-old children. Class 7 had worked on the topic 'heat' and class 5 on 'conservation' the term before the testing was carried out. Both classes revised their topics the week before the testing. Neither class 6 nor class 8 had received particular teaching on the topics. An extra set of booklets containing either the 'heat' questions but no passages, or the 'conservation' questions but no passages, was prepared for class 8.

The booklets were ordered using a table of random numbers and distributed in this order except for class 8 who had the booklets containing only the questions.

The analysis of the results did not reveal highly significant relationships between prior knowledge, the two levels of cohesion and comprehension.

Study 3. Post survey studies

Some work to explore the cohesion/comprehension relationship took place after the third collection of data. These studies were left until then as we wished for some purposes to present the passages in their complete form, that is, without deletions. A series of booklets was prepared which probed certain areas of the survey tests. In the main the study looks for the effects of the perception on various facets of comprehension.

Measurements concerning the basic tests, that is Ravens Matrices, NFER standardized reading tests, scores of the fiction and factual booklets together with scores from a set of specially prepared comprehension booklets were collected. These latter booklets contained test items to probe prior knowledge, inference, the comprehension of that part of the passage subjected to deletions, comprehension of passages not subjected to deletions and an overall comprehension score.

A significant correlation between the score on the booklets, both fact and fiction, and comprehension of the same passages was found.

As the results are concerned with 15-year-old children they will be discussed more fully in a later volume in the series that discusses the reading performance of secondary children.

Summary of in-depth studies

Taken together there is little doubt that the studies provide evidence that converges on the main study, giving it further validity. The first study shows that, among the information that is available to the children when responding to the Gap task, that deriving from cohesion beyond the sentence is dominant. The second study reveals that in the Gap task, levels of cohesion and prior knowledge do not appear to be highly significant. This would indicate that most of the information is again coming directly from the text. The third study provided confirmation that comprehension of the text was closely related to the Gap task.

Main survey data. Analysis technique 1

Gap analysis

This technique gives a series of measures. The first, consensus, gives an indication of the extent of the agreement within a group of children as to the response required by the gap filling task. This novel way of describing Gap results was derived from Information Theory which uses mathematical equations developed by communication engineers to calculate how much uncertainty there is in a communication situation. Uncertainty in this sense has a technical meaning and Anderson (1976) elaborated a way of using it to handle the data derived from cloze results. Essentially, it gives an estimate of the consensus there is in the responses given by the group. The consensus of the group is placed between the two extremes, that is, the case of every child providing a different response (no consensus) and every child having the same response (perfect consensus). As there are no occasions of complete agreement, consensus falls between these extremes and is expressed as a decimal fraction. The computer program written especially to handle the project data (Anderson 1981) first arranges the responses in their order of frequency and then gives the following series of measures for each cohesive tie:

Consensus (C)
Estimated Entropy (E) (A technical measure of redundancy)
No. of different responses (ND)
No. of Matches (exact replacement of author's word) (NM)
Proportion of these Matches (PM)
Proportion of Mismatches (PMM)

To illustrate the measurement of Consensus one of the items from an anchor passage is given in Table 4(1). (An anchor passage is one that appears in the booklets across all age groups. This was introduced at the beginning of the project, ahead of all the longitudinal data being assembled, to check that the work was going according to predictions. It also allows comparisons to be made across age range boundaries.)

Table 4(1) Consensus on the temporal conjunction 'then' according to chronological age

Age	Consensus	N
8 years	0.48	436
10 years	0.57	474
13 years	0.62	445

For this one deletion the measurement technique reveals the incremental progression expected as chronological age increases. The measure can be used also with groups of various sizes, e.g. a group within a school or a small class group. This versatility allows a series of comparisons to be made. For example, in Table 4(2) the children in School A achieved a higher level of agreement in their responses than those in School B. There were 21 different responses (ND) made by the 93 children in School A with some 43% (PM = 0.43) producing exact replacements. Whereas in School B, 114 children provided 34 (ND) responses with only 25% (PM = 0.25) giving the author's word as their response.

Table 4(2)   Consensus measure (c), number of different responses (ND) and proportion of exact responses (PM) for one item from two groups of ten-year-old children.

School	Consensus	ND	PM	N
A	0.53	21	0.43	93
B	0.42	34	0.25	114

A third illustration showing a comparison between the results of the three cohorts on three substitute items in Year 1 is given in Table 4(3). Taking Consensus (C) first, the expected increase with age on these three items is clearly observable. Although expected, the regularity of these and the other associated measures is impressive. When the number of different responses (ND) is inspected, the decrease expected with age also occurs.

The other measure, the exact replacement of the author's word (PM) is again consistent but the growth is very small compared with the level of agreement (C). In one case 'DID' the measures are unexpectedly low.

The computer program also performs basic statistics on the data and arranges it so that all the scores, those on the Standardized Reading Test, the Ravens Matrices and all the data from the Booklets, can be fed into and analysed by statistical programs on a main frame computer. There is also a facility for dividing the groups into thirds according to either their scores on the Raven's Matrices or the Standardized Reading Test.

Some of the results

As was indicated earlier the numbers of children, for whom complete results were available over the three years, declined. However, the final numbers remained high as will be seen below. To check on this loss, that is to make sure the children lost to the study would not unbalance the sample, a computer program was written to sort out and count for statistical purposes only the test details for those children who had been present for testing in each of the

Table 4(3) Quantitative data for anchor passage in Booklets 1 and 3 showing consensus (C), number of different responses (ND) and proportion of exact responses (PM) for 3 substitute items for 3 age groups.

	C	*ND*	*PM*
Substitute item 'one'			
Cohort A	.39	84	.27
Cohort B	.54	62	.27
Cohort C	.64	38	.36
Substitute item 'did'	*C*	*ND*	*PM*
Cohort A	.30	94	.7
Cohort B	.39	83	.19
Cohort C	.47	63	.34
Substitute item 'so'	*C*	*ND*	*PM*
Cohort A	.65	41	.64
Cohort B	.77	37	.76
Cohort C	.88	21	.89

Numbers in Cohorts:

Cohort A 8 years   436
Cohort B 10 years   476
Cohort C 13 years   445

three years. It was found that the sample had not been unduly affected. The results that follow are for these children.

It should be pointed out that the results reported below, that is those given by the quantitive measurement technique, use the author's word as the criterion. The reason for drawing this to your attention again is because of the drawbacks that are frequently noted with only counting the verbatim response or exact replacement of the author's word. The qualitative analysis, which follows these results, redresses this criticism by taking every response made by the children into consideration.

The mean scores of the children who have taken part throughout the three years are given by age, sex, and ability for all tests. For comparison each cohort is divided into thirds. The third of the group with the highest mean scores are designated the 'High band' and the lowest third, the 'Low band'. (A technical summary giving details of means, standard deviations, and standard errors is given in Appendix 2.)

A note about the methodological feature whereby children read the same booklets on three separate yearly occasions is perhaps required before the results are detailed. It is possible, of course, that there will be some kind of practice effect when the same materials are read in this way. However, this seems to have had little effect and was confirmed by the results of In-depth Study 1 above. Judicious questioning of a number of children was carried out also after the presentations and it was obvious that the children remembered very little of the detail of the passages.

For the following results, the cohorts were divided into 3 bands by NFER reading score. We compare the High and Low bands in each case.

Cohort A

Cohort A results are presented first in figures A1 (Ravens Matrices), A2 (Standardized reading tests), A3 Cohesion (fiction), and A4 Cohesion (factual).

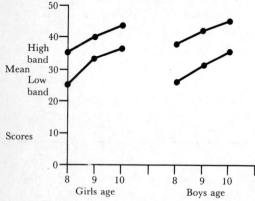

Figure A1   Cohort A. Ravens Matrices Results

The graphs of the mean scores for the Matrices test show little overall difference in ability on this non-verbal test between the boys and the girls. Although there were no significant differences, the girls in the low band had a slightly higher profile than the boys in that band at 8 and 9 years, but there was no mean score difference when they reached 10 years of age. It would

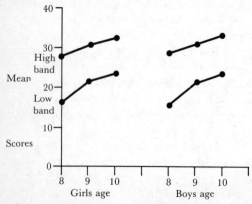

Figure A2   Cohort A. Standardized Reading Test Results

appear from this test that the groups were homogeneous and within the range of ability expected.

The first point to be made is that the ceiling of this standardized reading test was reached by both the girls and the boys in the high band. This may account for the tendency of the means to level off at 10 years. The steady progress of the low band children between 8 and 9 years is noticeable and although the progress is not so great they continue to improve up to 10 years.

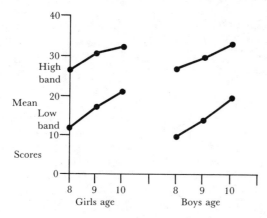

Figure A3 Cohort A. Results on Cohesion (Fiction) Tests

In these tests of textual cohesion (fiction) the high band boys and girls make progress up to 10 years with the boys making steady progress throughout. The girls in the low band also make steady progress up to 10 years, with the boys whose mean score was below that of the girls at 8 years showing considerable progress, particularly in the final year, when their graph becomes quite steep.

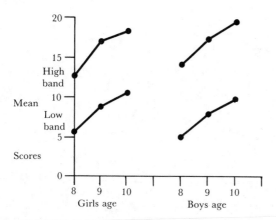

Figure A4 Cohort A. Results of Cohesion (Factual) Tests

Again these graphs show a picture of steady progress on textual cohesion (factual) tests between 8 and 10 years in both bands. The graph of the progress of the boys in the high band is at a particularly steep angle. However, it should be pointed out that when comparing these cohesion/genre results, the means in the factual graph are almost half those of the fiction graph.

Cohort B

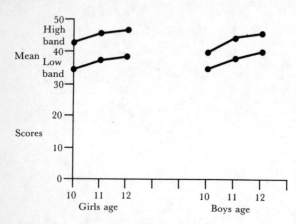

Figure B1   Cohort B. Ravens Matrices Results

As with the first cohort the result of this group's performances on the Matrices shows the composition of the group to be fairly homogeneous. The mean scores are higher by some 10 mean points than those of Cohort A. The boys in the high band group started with a lower mean score than the girls but there is little difference at 12 years of age.

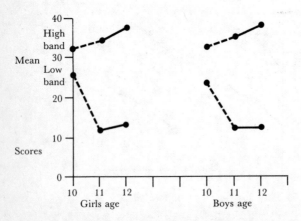

Figure B2   Cohort B. Standardized Reading Test Results

A little more explanation is required because, as mentioned above, these results for the data were collected first in the primary school and then the same children were followed into a number of secondary schools. In the primary school, when the children were 10 years old, a primary standardized reading test (NFER AD) was used and then, the following year on entering secondary school, a secondary reading test (NFER EH1) was given to them. It is interesting to note that, although this is a different group of children, the means of Cohort B in the first year of the project is virtually identical to the means of the corresponding groups in the final year of Cohort A. The next point of importance is the continuing steady progress of the high band children, boys and girls mean scores being the same. The change in tests appears not to have affected them at all. However, the lack of progress of the low band children is most marked. The mean scores on the secondary test are very low, the boys making no progress and the girls very little.

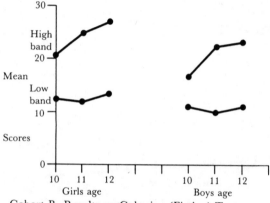

Figure B3   Cohort B. Results on Cohesion (Fiction) Tests

It is clear that the boys in the high band found the task more difficult than the girls, although both groups made progress, the boys particularly in their first year at secondary school. However, this progress was not maintained and their mean scores at 12 years was below that of the girls. The performance of

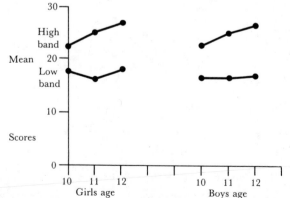

Figure B4   Cohort B. Results on Cohesion (Factual) Tests

the low band groups is very low. Little, if any progress is made by the boys and only a little by the girls.

The performance of the boys and girls in the high band reveals constant progress, whilst the boys in the low band make little or no progress whatsoever. The girls in that band after loosing ground make some progress but little above their original score at 10 years.

When these results are compared with the fiction results, the girls in the high band have almost identical profiles; however, the boys in the high band and both the girls and the boys in the low band have significantly lower scores on the fictional materials than on the factual.

Cohort C

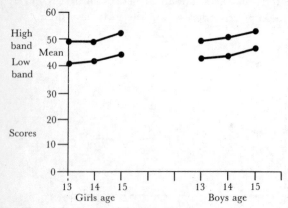

Figure C1 Cohort C. Ravens Matrices Results

Looking first at the Matrices results, apart from higher mean scores expected from the age differences involved, these results are comparable in homogeneity with the other two cohorts.

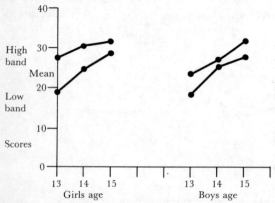

Figure C2 Cohort C. Standardized Reading Test Results

The graphs of the mean scores for both girls and boys in both bands show progress as far as this test is concerned. The mean score of the boys in the high band starts much lower than the girls in that band but by 15 years of age there is little difference in mean score. It is worth noticing also that although the girls have a higher mean score in the first year, their potential does not appear to be realized in that there is a slowdown in progress during the three years and the mean scores of the boys in the low group come close to the boys in the high band in the middle year but this is not maintained. However, the scores of the lower band are still low at 15 years, being less than the high band at 11 years.

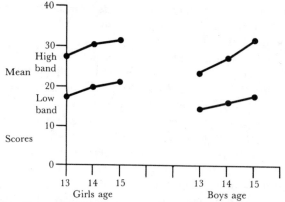

Figure C3 Cohort C. Results on Cohesion (Fiction) Tests

Again, as with the above results, it is important to notice the scales, which vary on these tests. In this case the scale runs form 0 to 40 compared with 0 to 30 in Cohort B. Taking this into account, the mean scores of the high band girls and boys in the first year are roughly comparable with those of the girls and boys in Cohort B in the final year. However, the low band boys and girls start at lower points and there is little progress during the three years.

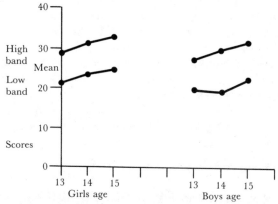

Figure C4 Cohort C. Results on Cohesion (Factual) Tests

The scale for these results is again 0 to 40 compared with that of the previous cohort. Whilst the higher band children continue to make progress, it is not until between the age of 14 and 15 years that the boys in the lower band, whose mean scores fall slightly between 13 and 14 years, begin to improve. There are signs of improvement in the mean scores of the lower group girls over the three years.

Summary

The results reveal that the children in Cohort A show constant improvement on the cohesion tests. Their mastery over their classroom books increases as their ages increase. There is a similar picture with the standardized tests which complement the cohesion test results.

It is not possible to have the same confidence about the results of the children in Cohort B. Here the situation described by Lunzer and Gardner (1979) is shown to be still the same. There is a standstill in the progress of the boys in the lower band with a flat graph for their reading of factual material and even lower mean scores on the fiction extracts. Both standardized tests were of the sentence completion type: the secondary one being a vocabulary test. It was clear that the lower band children's performance was seriously affected by this change in test, presumably as a result of the standardization process. In other words, it is possible that to achieve a spread of scores to delineate reading ability the test makers resorted to employing less frequently used vocabulary. The children in the high band do, however, surmount the problem of transition and continue to make progress on all tests. It is as though, having reached a certain threshold of performance in the primary school, they are able to maintain consistent progress in the secondary school when tackling the great variety of texts put before them.

The results of Cohort C children show improvement in the mean scores over the three years apart from the lower band boys whose scores on factual material appear to decline between 13 and 14 years. The fiction mean scores for the lower band are below those on the factual material.

Overall, and taking into account the findings of the Nottingham University project, the results indicate quite clearly that there is a need to give the teaching of reading greater attention throughout schooling. The results also point to ways in which this attention might be focussed. We will, however, postpone this until after a summary of the qualitative analysis of the cohesion results. This new analysis, which took every response made by the children into account, revealed new insights into children's reading development.

Main survey data. Analysis technique 2

To begin a description of this new analysis system, it is necessary to return to the notion of reading development. Although it might appear obvious, that is that reading develops to meet a variety of developmental and scholastic needs as children grow older, it is essential for teachers to appreciate the dimensions of these needs if they are to plan their teaching of reading effectively. As already mentioned the curriculum is geared to the increasing cognitive capacity of children as they mature. The dimensions of the reading materials are related to this and can be categorized by employing the concepts of genre and register and placed along a reading continuum. How this can be achieved in practical terms will be illustrated in Chapter 6 and 7.

The next requirement is to record what is meant by a continuum of reading. As soon as the concept is explained, most adult readers realize almost immediately that their own reading varies according to the type of text they are reading. It is obvious that all of us find that some materials are easier to read than others. For you, the reading of a favourite bedtime novel or book on a topic with which you are familiar, for example, will make lesser demands than a technical manual say, or a topic with which you are unfamiliar. And yet you would certainly qualify as a skilled reader. It is possible then, to imagine a continuity between the two in terms of your performance on the favourite novel or some other topic at one end of the continuum – to the right – and towards the opposite end would be your reading performance on, say, a technical manual or legal document with which you are decidedly unfamiliar. That is, although you are a skilled reader you will, nonetheless, be more familiar with some genres than others and perform accordingly. This leads us to propose a Reading Development Continuum (RDC) (Chapman 1983, 1985) which is embedded within the notions of cohesion and register or genre. The RDC is the framework for the qualitative analysis which we not go on to describe.

Turning to the children, their present level of ability for anyone reading performance is assessed by plotting their reading responses along a continuum. The location of each of these is decided by reference to a set of detailed response characteristics which clearly define each response's position along the continuum. When this was done in the initial development of the analysis, four main continuum positions were discovered, and these are shown by the diagram in Figure 7.

Using the RDC in this way enabled the research team to place each and every reading response obtained from the children according to its proximity to these four major positions. However, as this was being done, transitional areas that lie between these positions were found. When all the responses are so arranged and combined an overall assessment was made of the class or group, or sets of individual diagnostic profiles were produced. Alternatively the RDC can be applied to chapters of books, or indeed whole books, to assess their validity for learning.

The four positions referred to are based on the language description mentioned earlier in Chapter 2, Figure 2.

Recategorization

In the quantitative analysis the children's responses to the task were categorized according to the author's word. For the RDC, which we are calling a qualitative analysis, albeit a strictly controlled one, the responses are recategorized according to an extensive set of criteria which decide where the responses are placed.

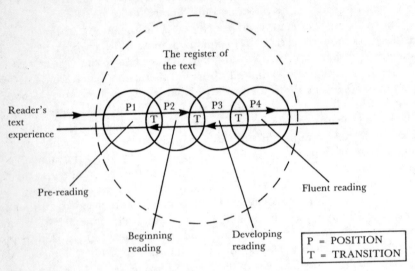

Figure 7   The reading development continuum

The continuum positions as shown in Figure 7, in summary form, are:

Position 1 (P1): the non perception of the clause element in which the deletion appears.
Position 2 (P2): the perception of the theme-rheme structure of the clause or sentence according to the rank ordering of systemic linguistics.
Position 3 (P3): the perception of cohesion and register of the text, but not the author's word.
Position 4 (P4): the replacement of the author's word.

For the longitudinal research each response from the frequency table provided by the associated quantitative computer program is recategorized according to a set of criteria listed below in Figure 8. In this way, the analysis eventually allows an interpretation at (1) individual deletion response level (per individual, class group, or whole geographical area) or (2) across a booklet and/or (3) both booklets, i.e. fiction and non-fiction, and/or (4) for three years. It is clear that this new assessment system has many applications and is particularly useful for evaluating the progress of children's reading performance on the reading materials actually in use for the school curriculum.

A Reading Development Continuum
(GAP Technique)

Position 1 (P1)	P1 Transition	Position 2 (P2)			P2 Transition
Pre-reading	E	Beginning reading (Clause Structure Perceived)			K
		H	I	J	
		Word Complex	Group Complex	Clause Complex	

Pre-reading

A. Omissions
B. Unrecognisable responses
C. Responses from V.P.F
D. Responses unacceptable in 1 Clause Element (1 CE)

P1 Transition — E

Response partially acceptable only: achieved by ignoring other word(s) in CE or by over-running punctuation and combining with word(s) from following CEs.

Position 2 (P2) — Beginning reading (Clause Structure Perceived)

H — Word Complex
Responses acceptable in 1 CE only (all other context ignored)

I — Group Complex
Responses acceptable in 2 or more CEs (all other context ignored)

J — Clause Complex
Responses acceptable in clause (complex) but lacking evidence of cohesion and register

P2 Transition — K

Responses showing evidence of cohesion and appropriate register but errors in lexicogrammatical structure(s).

Position 3 (P3)

Developing reading fluency

P

Responses indicate that clause structure perceived, cohesion perceived but achieved differently from author's, possible register errors of field, mode and tenor.

P3 Transition — R

Structure perceived. Register appropriate, cohesion perceived but not author's word.

Q

Responses indicate that clause structure perceived, register is appropriate but cohesion achieved differently from author.

Position 4 (P4)

Fluent Reading
Y

Criterion met (ie matched)

a) author's word

b) teacher's word

Figure 8 Summary of criteria for allocating responses

Plotting responses along the continuum

To illustrate how responses are plotted along the continuum, we show first how the responses of some of the 10-year-old children to one deletion are categorized. The piece of text involved (Figure 9) is taken from a history text

A Stuart Family in the Civil War

Sir Edmund Verney, was killed. He would not surrender the Standard, and his hand grasping it was cut off at the wrist. On the hand was this beautiful ring, given to him by King Charles. The ring holds a miniature of the King. After the battle the ring was returned to Sir Edmund's home, Claydon House, Buckinghamshire.

With the ring at Claydon House today are thousands of family letters. These are filled with the everyday doings of members of the family, at home and abroad, for over 500 years. There are 30,000 belonging to Stuart times alone. You will read passages from some of these letters on this page and the next.

Before the battle of Edgehill, Sir Edmund Verney wrote home:

'I pray have the carbines (guns) in reddyness for the defense of the house if need bee and gett powder and bullets ready: for I feare a time may come when Roags maye looke for booty in such houses.'

Many great houses were besieged and some burnt down during the Civil War. Sir Edmund's second son, Edmund, nicknamed 'Sir Mun', joined the King's ―――――――. His eldest brother Ralph sided with Parliament. When Sir Mun heard this news, he wrote to his brother:

'I am so much troubled to think of your being on the syde you are that I can write no more'.

What can you learn from this letter written by Thomas Verney, the third son?

'They living at Claydon' are subject to the affright of rude soldiers in rushing in all houres by day and by night.'

Troops of both armies were quartered at Claydon House during the war. When they left they often took horses and stores with them. Sir Ralph's wife wrote this about clearing up after the ―――――.

'I am so weary that I am scarce able to stand upon my legges trying to restore order.'

Apart from war, Ralph's sister Pen had other troubles. She writes of a:

'bruit of a husband who did cik me about the house.'

Perhaps ―――――― family has kept letters written during a war, or after a disaster, or from abroad. If ―――――― what facts can you discover from these?

Figure 9

from the secondary booklet about the Civil Wars in England. Three lexical cohesive chains realted to Kings, Family and Wars came together in and around the clause:

//'Sir Mun /joined/ the King's ——————.//

Position 1 (P1)

Responses allocated to P1 vary from the nil response (A) according to the definitions in Figure 8 above to a response that is completey unacceptable (D) as a snippet of English within the clause element containing the deletion. This is to say, the word(s) provided by the child, when taken with the words on either side of the deletion (or in case of the deletion falling at the end of the clause or sentence as here, the proceding word(s)) produce an unacceptable word complex. The amount of text for close inspection is next decided by using Goodman's (1975) notion of the extent of the visual peripheral field. That is the amount of text that is taken in, without us being aware of it, as the eyes move across the page. In his work this is two sentences above or below the point where a miscue occurs. In our research we use the position of the deletion on the page rather than a miscue. The definition is used in P1 also to examine those responses (C) that might simply be copied, as some were, directly from the surrounding text.

As noted above, the clause in question is,

//'Sir Mun /joined/ the King's ——————.//

The element with the deletion is:

/the King's ——————/.

The response must satisfy this construction first, *regardless of any other context whatsoever*. Responses such as 'had', 'was' and 'too' make unacceptable sequences in English; we cannot accept 'the King's had'; alternatively words like 'ring' and 'hand' are acceptable in this one clause element giving 'the King's ring' for example. As these latter responses are permissible they can be moved along the continuum into P2. As we worked like this in the research, a transition (T) phase appeared at this point. This occurred when the words immediately prior to the deletion were ignored and punctuation and other conventions of written text were disregarded. This occurred more often in the fiction texts and the following examples come from the well-known book 'Little House in the Prairie'. In this case two words '*Next morning*' were deleted as an example of conjunction at the beginning of a sentence. The extract from the Junior booklet was:

'How very kind of you', said the teacher looking at the two big red apples rather nervously. 'Thank you but you shouldn't.'

(The printing moves to the top of the page at this point.)

========= ============= , everyone in the class brought a big red apple for teacher. There were fourty-five children in the class and the fourty-five big red apples made the classroom look like Harvest Festival.

Responses to these deletions ranged widely, but among those indicating an attempt to complete a small piece of meaning were, 'of bothered', 'shout so', 'go telling', 'have let', 'blame him' and so on. If you now take the words immediately prior to the deletions, ignore the full stop, the new paragraph, and the move to the top of a new page, you get:

> you shouldn't of bothered,
> you shouldn't shout so,
> you shouldn't go telling etc.

Here there is an indication that the words have been understood and that a genuine attempt has been made to retain the genre and to make a little meaning. Of course, as soon as the words following the deletions are taken into consideration, these responses become unacceptable. Such responses as these are categorized at (E). There are thousands of responses in the project's data bank which, using this technique, indicate clearly and powerfully the growing textlinguistic ability of the children.

Position 2 (P2)

As we move along the continuum, it becomes possible to apply the rank scale of systemic linguistics, as outlined briefly in Chapter 2, so as to increase the context element by element in a controlled way. The response is rigorously checked as the context is increased through 'word complex', 'group complex' to 'clause complex'. In this procedure you must appreciate that we are advocating exactly the same 'intuition of the native language speaker' about language as is used by linguists to declare that some piece of language is, for example, grammatical or ungrammatical. Some would find this less than objective; however, it is widely accepted practice. In this way, responses to the extract from the history text, like 'sister', 'family' and 'table' are acceptable in the clause when it is taken in isolation and the rest of the context is ignored. In this you will note that this often involves accepting alternate meanings of the verb, in this case, 'join'. 'Sir Mun joined the King's sister'. 'Sir Mun joined the King's family' but, 'Sir Mun joined the King's table' for instance, is acceptable as well even if he were a carpenter!

As we move along the continuum the response is tested against increasing amounts of context. Responses now reveal the ability of the reader to perceive the theme/rheme nature of the clause. It would appear that the structural level is being processed successfully but not, necessarily, its cohesive value. As with P1/P2, there is a transition phase between P2 and P3, where there are indications that cohesion but not register is being perceived. This is the P2/P3 transition point. However, without the register requirement, the responses do not yet match the author's full text intention. Syntax, or theme/rheme requirement, have been satisfied but the author's semantic intention is not, as yet, fully perceived.

Position 3 (P3)

As the analysis enters the P3 area the characteristics governing decisions are whether the response is cohesive and finally whether it matches the genre of the text. Examination for the latter led to some very interesting discoveries regarding the perception of register, which we will summarize after the continuum has been explained in full.

The word deleted in the history text, *forces,* was from the 'war' cohesive chain and the responses could be clearly identified with this and the two other main threads of meaning, 'family' and 'royalty'. These response groupings are clearly shown by the Semantic Field diagram in Figure 10.

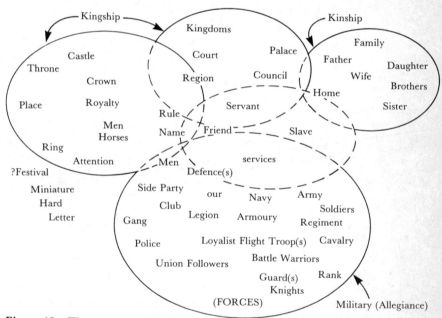

Figure 10 The responses of 807 children arranged into semantic fields cued by the three lexical cohesion chains: Kingship, Kinship, Military Allegiance

It was found that some children provided words that were cohesive, 'troops', 'guard' and 'Men' (all the King's horses and all the King's men'?) and do not offend the 'war' register requirement, but they are not the author's word. On the other hand the words 'union', 'police' and 'gang', whilst cohesive and in line with the meaning in general terms, in this particular context, a history text, are unacceptable from a register point of view.

Position 4 (P4)

And so to the fourth position where the verbatim response is placed. Here the author's word is held as the criterion and as such can be related back to the quantitative analysis. Some might protest here that the most frequent response, which was 'armies', should be counted as sufficiently near the author's intention to be accepted fully. However tempting this may be, particularly as every effort is made to give credit to the developing reader's performance, register considerations turned out to be as important an area of development as cohesion. This demanded that the author's actual word had to be maintained as the criterion. The correctness of this decision was reinforced during the work with the older secondary children when their curriculum was found to involve the comparison and contrasting of author style. Here the choice of word was most important and the discrimination required for this had to be developed. In addition, there is a parallel necessity for the scientist to be able to read with complete accuracy. It becomes too easy to accept less than the criterion. Furthermore, as we will see it was found that accuracy, in term's of nearness to the author's word, was clearly a major characteristic of the high band readers. (Examples of responses allocated to categories appear in Appendix 5.)

Some results

There were many interesting findings for teachers from the research. Some broad outlines will be given here but such is the amount of detail gathered more will be given in later volumes according to the age range involved.

The reading progress of children aged 8 to 10 years

The histogram in Figure H1 shows the performance of 293 children over the three years of the research programme arranged according to the continuum. You should recall that these are the children for whom we have complete records. The histograms are set out so as to show the perception and non-perception of cohesion clearly. The two position along the continuum where the responses lacking of cohesion are placed are shown below the line as negative amounts. The responses allocated to positions P3 and P4 are located above the line as 'cohesion perceived'.

The four continuum positions are recorded along the horizontal axis with the age of the cohort at that time, that is at 8, 9, and 10 years. The vertical axis has the percentage mean scores marked along it.

The progression of the children's reading is depicted quite clearly by these histograms which take into account every response. There are many

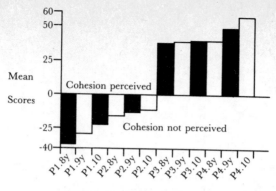

RDC Positions at 8, 9, and 10 years.

Figure H1   Histogram of 293 Children's Reading Progress over 3 Years

interesting features shown by the analysis. First, there is the step-like decrease in the responses that are at P1 and P2 as the age of the children increases. However, although there are a considerable number of P1 and P2 responses, there are just as many responses at the P3 and P4 positions. The most important gain in the cohort's reading performance occurred during the third year of the project. The children were then 10 years of age, with some already having reached 11 years. If you combine the P3 and P4 responses as an indication of the ability to gain the full, or nearly the full meaning of their curriculum texts (the cohorts mean score near the 90 per cent range), then this reflects an encouraging situation for the teaching of reading in the junior schools, at least as far as the children in this sample are concerned.

As well as showing the move along the continuum with age, if the cohort is divided into three as was done in the quantitative measure, we find that the children in the high band have results that are categorized as being in the P3 and P4 areas. The low bands' responses are correspondingly bunched to the left of the RDC with more responses at P1 and P2 than at P3 and P4. This demonstrates again that the characteristic of the fluent reader is undoubtedly the ability to perceive the cohesive links efficiently. The distinctive characteristics of the high band reader is accuracy in terms of nearness to the author's intended meaning. This is demonstrated in the individual profiles which we discuss next.

Individual profiles

Mention now needs to be made of the generation of individual profiles; samples of these in graphic form can be seen in figures 11, 12 and 13. Here the characteristic shapes of the graphs for high, middle and low performers over two years can be seen quite clearly. The figures alon the x axis 1, 2, 3, 4 are the four positions, K is the cohesion point.

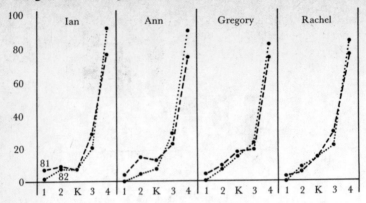

Figure 11   Individual RDC profiles (A) high performers

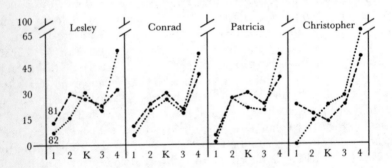

Figure 12   Individual RDC profiles (B) medium performers

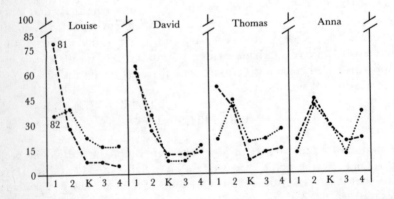

Figure 13   Individual RDC profiles (C) low performers

The profiles can be of diagnostic value to teachers who can be made aware of the overall progress of individual children according to their performance relative to the RDC. In this way their teaching can be made more principled and, as it is based on the child's own learning materials, much more effective. To illustrate this aspect of the research we give profiles of the progress of a very poor reader over three years. This was one of the children whose class teacher did not want excluded from the research. The profiles of his performance on fictional and factual texts are given separately.

The first profile is of this boy's performance at 8 years on the fictional texts. It shows that the preponderance of the responses are at the P1(D) stage. This

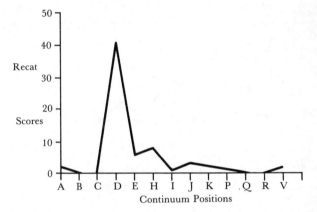

Figure 14   Analysis of RDC responses of 8 year old poor reader (1038). Yr. 1. Fiction

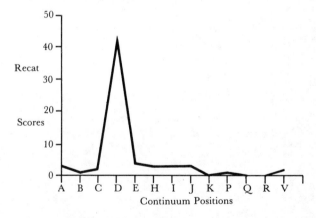

Figure 15   Analysis of RDC responses of 8 year old poor reader (1038). Yr. 1. Factual

means that he is inserting words that are unacceptable in the very restricted context of a clasue element. It is important to notice, however, that there are few non-responses, none that are unintelligible and none copied from the immediate vicinity of the deletion. There are a few at the transition point at E and a few at H and to a lesser extent at J, indicating that there are a few successful attempts to make meaning, but in a very limited way. The performance on the factual text is even more depressed. There are more responses coded as P1 and even fewer at P2.

If we now consider the fiction profile a year later, that is at 9 years of age, there is a marked decrease in the number of 'D' responses, the number at 'I'

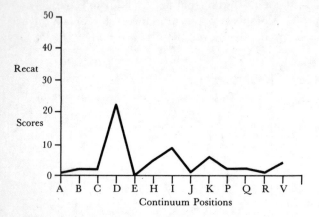

Figure 16   Analysis of RDC responses of 9 year old poor reader (1038). Yr. 2. Fiction

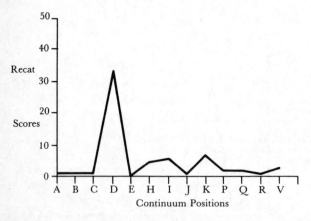

Figure 17   Analysis of RDC responses of 9 year old poor reader (1038). Yr. 2. Factual

in the P2 position has increased and there are now some that show attempts to give a cohesive replacement; there is even one or two answers at P4. There has been a performance gain such that the reader is monitoring his reading and not entering so many unacceptable words. He is also managing greater amounts of context and attempting to provide the cohesive linkages. Again the performance on the factual material is not so good. Here there is a greater number of 'D' responses, not so many at 'I' but there are slightly more at 'K' and 'V' which signifies verbatim responses.

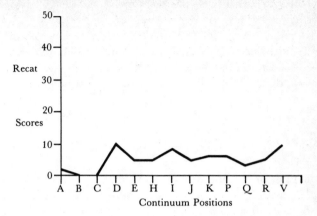

Figure 18   Analysis of RDC responses of 10 year old poor reader (1038). Yr. 3. Fiction

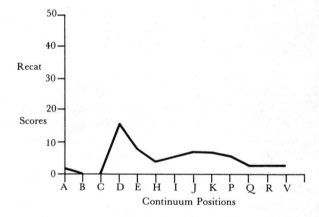

Figure 19   Analysis of RDC responses of 10 year old poor reader (1038). Yr. 3. Factual

The graph of the performance on the fictional texts at 10 years of age shows the gains detected at 9 years have continued. We now have relatively few responses at 'D' and there is an increase in all other categories along the continuuum with verbatim responses continuing to rise. If we compare this with the performance on factual texts shown in the final graph we see that this is at a lower level than the fictional. However, it is improving.

We will only comment briefly here on these profiles as we will be turning to them again during the teaching aspects that follow in Chapters 6 and 7. We will note, however, that there is a great deal of potential in conceiving of reading as a language process. Such an emphasis does not exclude cognitive aspects as we will note in the next chapter, but it does have the advantage of providing a basis for the continuum concept just described. This, in turn, has made it possible to uncover something of the level of this boy's textlinguistic knowledge that will support the development of his reading and writing.

In terms of the specific set of profiles, you will be able to see clearly how this boy's reading has developed in terms of the books provided for him in junior school. You will note that the RDC makes it possible to diagnose the strengths and weaknesses in the boy's performance in some considerable detail. He can now be tutored so as to build on his strengths using the same books as the rest of his peer group, thus avoiding the embarrassment of being singled out by the use of special materials.

Summary of findings

1.   One of the most important insights provided by the research project is the validity given to the perception of cohesion and register or genre as important elements in the reading process. These are new dimensions not sufficiently acknowledged in other accounts. (This relates directly to the first aim of the project).

2.   A further and related outcome of the research was the shift in perspective on the reading process that became necessary when the results were examined using both analysis procedures. It was no longer satisfactory to think in terms of reading ages or quotients.

The results obtained from charting the reading growth of nearly 1,500 children between the ages of 8 and 15 years show clearly that such concepts are misleading. When their reading responses were plotted year by year it became clear that reading ability was best accommodated along a continuum that stretches from the non- or erroneous perception of the meaning of given selections of texts to the accurate perception of the author's intended meaning. It is important that any discussion of baseline reading includes the notion of a continuum. Other factors such as critical and aesthetic appreciation can then be taught with a greater chance of success.

3.   Most assessment systems use some form of specially contrived reading materials as a basis for testing. These are either pieces of text written by the test makers, pieces of text that simulate activities or texts that have been adapted in some way. In whatever way this may be done it remains at a distance from the real reading situation in school. This project took a new stance and used the books chosen to support the school curriculum as its basic reading material.

4.   Following on from this is the devising of the reading development profile system which allows the recording of an individual child's progress with these materials, or, if used with groups, the reading development of classes in a school over periods of time.

5.   The delineation of text types, crude though they may be in this research, illustrated the need for children to meet different types of text early in their school careers. Only then will they have a chance to maintain progress when

faced with the full range of material presented to them in their education.

6.   It was clear from the results that there was a serious problem in the reading achievement of children in the lower band, and possibly also the average readers, after entry into secondary schooling.

7.   Further insights as to the nature of misperception were given when the responses to deletions were examined where cohesive chains met or were juxtaposed. For example, when one of the three chains in the excerpt from the history text used as an exemplar above was interrupted and the children asked to replace the ties, the resulting responses could be allocated to a number of definite semantic fields. It is interesting to align the responses to the chains that probably gave rise to them. These clearly indicate various levels of meaning perception and mis-perception and are important for both diagnostic purposes and for text design.

8.   Finally at this stage in reporting, there is the development of teaching strategies made possible due to the closeness of the research design to classroom practice. An outline of suggestions for teaching follows in Chapters 6 and 7.

CHAPTER 5

Towards a framework for rethinking and teaching reading

The framework put forward here draws on the OU research and the descriptive linguistics of Halliday mentioned in the previous chapters. The objective is to provide a theoretical background to enable teachers to rethink their teaching of reading and, as we will see, their language work in general.

We review a theory of reading first, and then outline the context of reading in schools by defining the concept of reading development. These proposals are then put into a perspective that will provide an introduction to the development of classroom practice.

This account of reading is not the early version that regarded reading as an entirely 'top-down' or meaning governed process. While we would agree with informed opinion (Anderson *et al.* 1985) that reading is basically a meaning getting process, we conceive it to be an interactive one which also involves bottom-up, or what are sometimes termed, text-driven factors. We have noted the nature of systemic grammar and you may have realized its affinity with 'bottom-up' processing through its constituent analysis procedures (Hoey 1983). However, it is the other features of Halliday's language description that causes the theory to differ significantly from previous reading theories like those of Goodman. The new definition proposed has an entirely different linguistic background and, as you will have gathered by now, has some support from empirical results. In essence we have a psycho socio-linguistic theory for reading and writing. Such a title is, however, inelegant and as the linguistic description proposed embodies the social semeiotic nature of language, we have not adopted any of the terms usually met. However, the account is based on psychological as well as linguistic theory.

The psychological part of the theory is informed by Vygotsky's (1962) views, particularly the close interrelationships between language, thought and concept development. We have noted that the processing of the cohesive links has psychological implications which are extended therefore to include text processing and metacognition. Schema theory involves, as we noted, the organization of the storage of concepts about the world in memory. In an earlier book (Chapman 1983), some of the detail of the background knowledge within one particular schema was indicated by Charniak's (1972) lists of the knowledge we have stored regarding a simple everyday concept, that of a child's piggy-bank and saving. When the detail is spelt out (see Appendix 4 for a copy of the list) the extent of what we already know about the concept is quite surprising. When such a schema is alerted by reading the name, or some other associated factor, our attempts to comprehend the text is informed by this prior (to reading) knowledge.

Although knowledge schema have been called 'The building blocks of cognition' (Rumelhart 1980), in our opinion they are certain to have an associated language schema or the schema itself has language built into it. This is a very important addition to most schema descriptions which hardly consider language and has implications for those theorists who attempt to separate cognitive from linguistic aspects of language.

As well as schema effects, the reader is also influenced by the structure of the text. We noted in the review of text structure research that processing can be thought of as operating at three levels within the structure: micro and macro-propositional levels and top-level. Halliday's proposal of texture (cohesion and register) can be fitted into this framework. The cohesive ties link the semantic or meaning elements, or propositions at the micropropositional level within the sentence and between the sentences, while some, the conjunctives, are more observed at the macropropositional, or paragraph level. Other linguistic input, the register effects, are more likely to be perceived at the top-level. However, these features are interactive, hence reading one word, given an appropriate schema, will alert an appropriate register. As we have noted if you read the word astronaut, for example, a number of associations spring readily to mind and become presupposed. Further you will find that a more general word like capsule takes on a particular meaning by further cues from the context. That is, the first group of word associatons becomes refined as the reading proceeds. There is no need to pursue this further for you to appreciate that there are strong connections between the psychological and linguistic theory. Certainly it provides a far sounder explanation for the processes of anticipation than those proposed by others who attempt to keep the two facets artificially separate.

Cohesive ties and chaining

We go on to elaborate further how the cohesive tie system and the proposals for chaining the ties operates during reading. As we have noted cohesive ties are said to work according to a mechanism called presupposition. In this the onset of any one tie is said to foreshadow its closure. In reading terms we could say that the reader, having perceived the beginning of a tie, will anticipate that it will be connected or tied up before long. This expectation comes from the reader's linguistic awareness of how language works. So, for example, in a story it is customary for the characterers to be named at the outset (unless the author is seeking to make some point of emphasis), and readers' knowledge of English leads them to anticipate that pronouns will be met when those characters are next referred to in the story rather than their names. Due to the many options available for making meaning and the creativity of writers in exploiting those options, the continuity effect can be achieved in many ways. However, presupposition is the basic mechanism of the system. In technical terms the mention of the antecedent causes the pronoun to be presupposed. Furthermore, it follows that the pronoun cannot be fully understood without being tied to the name. And you should note here that when reading, the reader is moving forward through the text and you should not be confused by the linguistic notion of anaphora and referral back to the antecedent. It is only when we reach an ambiguity in the anaphoric situation that we actually look back to what has gone before (Just and Carpenter 1977); in normal reading the process is a movement forward.

You will have seen examples of lack of completed ties in children's writing where the child expects you to know for whom the pronouns stand without their antecedents – the names to which they refer – being clearly stated. This is a clear demonstration of the way in which children have to absorb the textlinguistic conventions which differ from those of speech. The research of Pettegrew (1981) shows that it takes a while for children to learn to write endophorically (make their connections within the text) rather than exophorically (that is, make links to the outside context).

The presupposition factor in fluent reading is the theoretical base for the profiling system being proposed later. This system was rigorously validated during the OU Perception of Cohesion project reviewed in the previous chapter. To construct a reading profile the ends of a series of ties were removed and children asked to replace them. It was argued that if they were able to do this then it was evidence of their ability to perceive the tie and that they were able to knot the text together and hence make meaning of the whole text.

Chaining and metacognition

It is necessary to remember that cohesive ties are chained through a text and it is this chaining that enables the reader to keep track of the persons and events in, for example, a story. It also applies in a similar way to non-fiction materials where the chains relate to a topic. As well as the ability to effect the closure of a tie, it is also necessary to follow the chains and this involves a monitoring process that keeps the reader on the right track. It is proposed that this monitoring is one of the metacognition processes that were briefly reviewed earlier. It has often been observed by teachers that children sometimes lose their way in a story, and here is one of the explanations for this: they may become confused by competing chains which weave through the text or simply miss a link and become lost. We have then cohesive tie anticipation and chain monitoring as integral parts of the reading process, but we have another term to define more adequately before we complete this section, that is reading development.

Reading development

To teach and assess reading, it is necessary to have some idea of what is expected of children's reading at specific times in their school careers. The level of reading is clearly dependent on the demands of the school's curriculum. For it is the needs of the curriculum, which is decided mostly by the level of children's cognitive development at various ages, that requires reading to develop. It is this imperative therefore, that makes it necessary for teachers to form a clear concept of reading development. They need to be able to envisage the level of reading sophistication required by the texts they and others choose for learning.

The term reading development, which is so often used, is however, rarely defined. We will make a start to remedy this by first identifying the purposes of reading.

1. Reading for personal growth and pleasure, i.e through literature and other types of fictional or non-fictional material.
2. Reading for use in the world:
   a) in the community so as to survive as a citizen,
   b) in the school for the attainment of knowledge, i.e, broadly, through reading junior information texts, secondary text-books and other factual material.
   c) later, as an adult, to be an active, independent learner.

Obviously these are rough categories that overlap according to the purposes of reading; it can be pleasurable, for instance, to read for knowledge as well as literary purposes. The divisions made here and in other practical areas are for convenience for organization and will be refined as we proceed.

We have neither appreciated, nor has it been possible until recently, to describe the vast range of reading matter that support these aims apart from simple cataloguing. Fortunately, we can now begin to describe the characteristics of this material by utilizing the concept of texture, that is cohesion and register or genre, that we have been discussing.

We noted earlier in Chapter 2 that this linguistic perspective posits that you cannot understand text without knowing about the social and cultural context in which it occurs. The three features of the context of situation are field (what the language is about), tenor (the way roles and relationships are expressed) and mode (the channel of the communication). To this register dimension we added the associated term, genre.

Summary of theoretical aspects

In the first part of the chapter we have assembled from research some of the significant factors relating to reading that are now available and have combined these with a linguistic base drawn from the work of Halliday and his associates. In this brief theoretical resumé, we have noted the importance of texture, that is cohesion and register and the accompanying psychological process of prediction and monitoring.

Reading assessment

In the second part of this chapter we continue the discussion of reading by demonstrating how some of the principles can be put into practice. We look first at one of the obligations allotted to teachers and schools, that of assessment.

Assessment is probably one of the most controversial practices in education. Yet it is taking place continually whether by formal or informal means. In order to ascertain how well schools are doing their jobs, schools themselves often choose to administer commercially produced tests,or, in the case of the DES, national standards are assessed by the APU. Informally, either by prepared means or in the process of teaching, children's progress is being summed up in their day to day activities. Knowing how pupils are progressing is an unescapable part of teaching. Additionally, parents have the right to know how well their children are doing in school. This being so it is encumbent upon all involved to make sure it is as efficiently done as possible.

We propose here that reading assessment, to be realistic and meaningful to others both in and out of school, needs to be carried out on the curriculum materials chosen by teachers for their age, or subject, group. This has to be emphasized on two counts. Firstly, one of the prime educational aims must be to produce independent learners. All our children need to be able to continue learning throughout life except for that small number who are mentally incapable of reading. It is impossible to imagine how such life-long learning will not contain a variety of books both formal and informal. Children ought to be introduced to a wide range of these types at school. We trust also that they will have more than community survival skills and will be able to read for enjoyment. The second important point is that to produce reading assessment materials that do not bear directly on the reading done in schools is in danger of producing a false picture of reading attainment. This is because there are clear signs in the OU research of the 'retreating from print' referred to by the research team from Nottingham University. In the secondary schools the need to read continuous text is circumvented by the production of an incredible number of worksheets. These are made up of a number of single sentences of short paragraphs, alternatively and/or in addition to, teacher produced worksheets. Knowledge is transmitted orally without recourse to the printed medium. Secondly, to simulate the reading materials can give an erroneous impression, mostly by underrating the scale of difficulty of most textbooks. This is because to simulate or adapt materials is likely to remove reading problems faced in 'real' texts. Secondly, and almost certainly, the process of simulation or adaption involves specially constructed reading materials to provide a test bed for the assessment procedures, else why simulate or adapt, why not use the real thing? These factors are apparent in the APU assessment materials and because of the dubious use of questioning techniques, could mean that the standard of reading in schools is being overestimated nationally. Unfortunately, there is little, if any, theoretical base for the APU's reading assessment procedures to discuss. This is clear from the Director's framework for assessment (Gorman 1986).

The proposals for assessment advocated here have three characteristics. They are thought of first as being part of teaching. Secondly, they are based directly on curriculum materials and thirdly they involve the theoretical perspective outlined above.

Assessing reading demands

To assess reading development using these principles, we first have to ask the question, what are the significant register and genre differences between the texts being read in school? We can then go on to analyse examples of these register variations for their cohesive properties.

Two main operations are required to begin a survey of the reading demands of your curriculum.

A. First, take all the reading material used for one age group and divide them into fiction and non-fiction using a simplified Dewey system.

Second, grade them according to how far the text moves from the familiar language of the child's home or early reading stories through so-called 'good' children's literature to heritage literature.

Third, grade them according to how technical the information is from the simple content books for infants to the junior information books.

When this is done you will probably be surprised at the range of reading materials in any one class or group. In this practical way you will have gained also first hand knowledge of the extent of the register demands of your school's books. You will also note that it requires a continuum of reading skills for your readers who will differ widely in their ability to cope with the range.

B. Next the individual books need examining for the cohesive chains that carry the threads of meaning that run through them. We are not suggesting the analysis of every book! Rather take a main thread of meaning and follow this through for its cohesive qualities. In addition a useful refinement is to note the tie-distances within those chains.

You are now in the positions to choose typical passages that are representative of those texts and duplicate them. Here you must be careful not to infringe any copyright regulations that may govern copying of pages from books.

The result of this initial preparation is the basis of reading assessment in terms of your own curriculum, not on some test constructer's simulation of what children should be capable of reading but in terms of your school's curriculum priorities. This collection of materials will last as long as you are using those books, and after the initial work, which will be demanding, serve for many years. Any new books that are purchased can be similarly analysed and added to the assessment material.

There are many spin-offs from the procedure; teacher knowledge of the books in school, appreciation of reading problems and an overall view of the reading demands being made by the curriculum. The profiles to be described next are designed to be used as diagnostic tools to estimate strengths and weaknesses of reading those school texts.

A new profile system

How to create a profile of:

a group (class or school)
an individual

It seems so obvious to say that children need to understand the books they read for the goal of all reading is comprehension. Indeed some go so far as to say that reading is comprehension. However, many appear to be reading with understanding but they are not really doing so with accuracy. And there is an important point here. Teachers and parents do not wish to hold up the development of their children's reading by constant attention to accuracy, but accuracy becomes a necessary criteria as children advance through the school system. A balance has to be kept, but this is the product of reading; we also need to know what goes on during reading. This process we call comprehending. We can keep track of comprehending by looking for tie completion along the cohesive chains.

Interrupting the chains

It is necessary first to identify a typical passage of some length – at least a page, preferably more – for the cohesive tie analysis. You have had a summary of ties given earlier in Chapter 2, but if you have problems recognizing them there are a number of examples of the different cohesive ties in Reading Development and Cohesion (Chapman 1983) and you should be able to identify sufficient for your profiling purposes from these. A further source of guidance is in Halliday and Hasan (1976) but this is often found to be too technical for many teachers.

The next step, having selected a number of cohesive ties for deletion is to take out a link from a prominent chain, one that is carrying the author's main thread of meaning. Continue with this procedure until you have six to eight deletions per page. You will not need more.

It is advisable now to have a trial run with some of the materials and you should ask your group or class to fill in the blanks. Make quite sure that they read through the text first so as to establish the context. They should not be hurried to complete, let them proceed at their own pace. You can then count this as a practice run and ask the children to discuss their responses with you or each other.

Having prepared assessment versions for the main books or other reading materials used for your curriculum purposes, you will have sufficient data from the children's completion of the sample to devise a profile for the class or for each individual.

Analysing the responses

Using the trial data you will now be able to try out the analysis procedures. In Chapter 4 there is a set of criteria for you to apply to the responses you have collected. You will note that each category is identified by a letter of the alphabet. In this version of the profiling system we have A to cover the non-response and V the replacement of the exact word used by the author.

The results of this gap-filling exercise can now be plotted on a profile sheet consisting of four columns, one for each continuum position. A line can be drawn across the page to represent the continuum as in the diagram in Figure 7. If the page is then divided up into thirds for the three terms, you will be able to watch the progress along the continuum lines. You will now be ready to look at the detailed use of your rudimentary profile sheet in the following chapters.

CHAPTER 6

Teaching reading in the infant school

Some background preliminaries

We have discussed a theoretical framework for the teaching and assessment of reading in the previous chapter. However, before we detail a programme for teaching reading using this, we need to draw together other factors that impinge on children prior to their reception into school. These refer to the children's family background and the wholeness of language.

In many ways the two co-occur as is clear from the thinking and research into emergent literacy. We noted earlier that literacy is conceived to be developing from the earliest months of the child's life and that this perspective has important implications for later schooling. We have learned also that language is a symbolic system, a system of signs, and if you bear this in mind in your observations of very young children you will begin to notice even at the baby stage that children are already symbol users. A personal observation might help to illustrate what is meant by these early indications of literacy. An eight to nine-month-old baby was attracted by horses in a field near her home. When taken to see them, her parents made the usual tongue clicking noises that many associate with horses. On returning home some while later, her attention was drawn to a picture of the heads of two horses. On seeing them the child replicated the clicking sounds heard earlier, spontaneously. The point of this is that not only had the child remembered the sound/animal association but has subsequently recognized a picture of that animal and provided the sound symbol accurately. Although this is anecdotal it does serve to illustrate how early the beginnings of literacy development are and remind us that the years before schooling are not devoid of experiences that are very pertinent to literacy development. These early beginnings should not be ignored for it is now clear, if it was not so already, that the child is not a tabula rasa, a clean state, but has begun to learn how to be literate before entering school.

The second facet of the approach being advocated concerns reading within a whole language setting. We need to be reminded that emergent literacy concerns language as a whole process. For, mostly due to earlier pedagogical practices, the two language modes of reading and writing, for example, were often timetabled separately and taught apart. The modes were thought of as individual entities, each needing separate practice. Even today, many teachers are used to attending to the four modes, speaking, listening, reading and writing separately. However, in the programme that follows we propose that children are taught in such a way, and sufficiently often for the unity of language to be maintained. Although children will undoubtedly need to practise the individual skills of reading and writing, there has to be direct teaching sessions that involve the relationships of the four modes.

School–parent relationships

There is hardly any need to say that contact with parents needs to be made well before the child actually begins full-time attendance at school. How this is handled depends on the policy of the school but preliminary visits are most important, not only from the individual child's point of view but also for the opportunity they afford the teacher to observe individual children. We have become accustomed to regarding these introductory sessions as ways of avoiding emotional upsets and this indeed has an over-riding importance. However, we must also utilize the opportunities these visits present for the beginning of an informal assessment of the child's level of developing literacy in that non-prying way that is characteristic of the professional teacher. Approaches to parents can be made that will enable you to learn of the experiences the child has had of toddler and playgroups in the neighbourhood as well as features in the home that contribute to the development of literacy in natural conditions.

It is obvious, especially from the research into the effects of home school cooperation with reading activities, that full parent-teacher cooperation enhances children's learning and more specifically their literacy development. Parents have one great advantage over the teacher: they can usually arrange for a one-to-one situation on a regular daily basis to give practice in reading and writing. Furthermore, the very fact that they are cooperating gives the school added backing and demonstrates to the child that they value what the teacher values. While many teachers aim at individual teaching there is nothing to replace the benefits that active parent cooperation can contribute to this. It is true that there are some parents that will, for many reasons, be unable to handle these proposals, but they are in the minority and this should not detract from the programme envisaged here.

A teaching programme outline

The programme for teaching will be discussed in two sections, one for the early infant years and the other in the next chapter for the years in the junior school.

The structure of all the proposed programmes involves answering six basic questions:

1. What aspects of literacy need developing?
2. What knowledge is now available to help?
3. What teaching strategies can be designed to meet the needs?
4. What teaching methods are required?
5. How might the teaching be evaluated?
6. How might the pupils be evaluated?

The early years

Assessing the needs

We have already begun the discussion of the child's entry to school when his or her level of development is informally assessed and these features will guide your formulation of the particular needs of your group. Having these in mind we concentrate now on aspects of literacy development that pertain specifically to reading. We do this by first presenting the reading assessment structure that will be common to all ages covered in the rest of this and other volumes. This structure is based on the concept of the reading development continuum (RDC).

As we have mentioned earlier in Chapter 4 the continuum stretches from the absence of formal reading skill to the ability to read a great variety of texts fluently. As literacy development is emerging almost from birth then children must already be absorbing knowledge of these processes from their culture and acquiring the beginnings of the concepts of reading and writing. To decide how much they have achieved is the first assessment requirement. To help you codify these we show you how to plot them on the RDC.

The RDC is thought of as having four positions viz pre- or emergent-reading, (that is, before the child has demonstrated the ability to read a few words), developing reading, extending reading and fluent reading. We begin then to apply the principles of the continuum to the early stages of reading in the infant school or kindergarten.

Position 1. (P1) Pre- or Emergent-reading

It should be pointed out that although the tasks that follow should be as accurately assessed as possible, it is intended that they should be carried out in normal classroom conditions and built into the day to day activities of the group. On no account should they acquire a test type aura because children need to develop, if they have not already done so, a love of books.

The first task involves checking the level of each child's literacy. To do this we focus initially on the ability of a child to produce orally, and recognize in print, two or more closely associated words in context. It should be emphasized that this is not two associated words in isolation but two or more embedded in a text. The type of associations we have in mind is called collocation by linguists and consists of words that frequently co-occur. To ascertain the oral production of such collocates, it is easy when reading to children in a natural story session to pause after a word that is closely associated with another. The child is expected to produce the following word. For example, bus (pause) stop, fish and (pause) chips, hammer and (pause) nails are common combinations. Also involved is the ability to complete a few words of a sentence from its underlying grammatical structure. If the children are able to do this orally and also recognize such words in print in the context of a story or other text which the teacher is reading to them, then they are predicting and are at least within the transition stage between positions 1 and 2 and the assessment can be continued to see if they are further along the continuum into P2, the developing reading position. We will come to this after providing for the children who are recorded as being no farther along the continuum than position 1. The criteria to apply are, if the child produces a word that is unconnected with the word given or if the child is unable to recognize a printed word or recognizes it wrongly when you have read 'the words leading up to it, then the reading is at P1. And again, if the word(s) given is out of context then the reading is still at P1.

Teaching children at Position 1

1. What needs developing?
From this assessment you will be able to plan to meet the needs of those children who display the characteristics of P1 reading. These needs will be met by providing the same type of experiences that children from 'literate' homes have enjoyed.

2. What knowledge is available?
Some of the need can be met from the knowledge we have gained about children's concepts of print and language, including the language teacher's use to teach reading (Reid 1984, Downing 1970 and 1976, and Clay 1972). In this the teacher has to provide much of the enrichment that some parents have already given about books and print before schooling begins. The over-riding concept to be attained is as true for these children as it is for all, that 'those black squiggles on the page carry a message, they mean something'. There are a number of other, for many taken for granted, aspects that may need attention, like which is the front of a book, where we start to read, turning

pages, following lines from left to right and from top to bottom of the page. What a letter is and what a word is, how pictures or illustrations are related to the print and so on. These will probably need attending to as will the language of books.

Two further major factors are supplied by the notions of schemata and, following Vygotsky's (1962) notion of the 'zone of proximal development', to teach the child's next stage of development. In this children need to have developed a number of schemata for the type of literacy activities planned. Because there is a suspicion that there has been a decline in bedtime story telling or reading, some may need to develop story schemata, others may need vocabulary extension, others still may need a knowledge base for the non-fiction texts they will be meeting. These are areas that need planning within the many other activities that are practised under other headings, for example, natural history and environmental studies, so that present schemata are developed or new ones, which we understand may need rich experiences to establish, added. As we saw earlier, Vygotsky presented two concepts which we consider valuable for the practice of teaching. These are firstly, the close affinity of language and thought. The two factors, the cognitive and the linguistic, although having separate roots nonetheless come together early in the child's life and thereafter are considered inseparable. Hence, it is extremely important to assist children's vocabulary development alongside their concept or schema development. The second insight is particularly valuable for teaching strategies. Your sights should be fixed beyond the child's present development to the next position on the continuum. In this the child can reach out to the next stage with the help of adults. The important things to remember then are the wholeness of language and its unity with knowledge schemata and the next stage of development.

3.   The teaching strategy
We begin this section with a quote:

> It is universally recognized that, when children come to school, there is a wide gap between those who are best prepared and those who are least prepared for school learning. The question then is how to close the gap *early*, for if it is not soon closed it will widen. This is the way with gaps of such a kind.
>
> (Donaldson 1978:96)

The strategy to be adopted will have a twofold aim, to give the enrichment that others in the class may have had already in the home to those who need it, and to help the child reach forward to the next stage by giving support. However, as there are such variations in development, some children who have a rich literary environment may still not have absorbed all of these features. The methods that follow are suggestions for the type of teaching approach necessary that will help to alleviate the problem or close the gap by immersing the children in literacy.

4. The methods

(a)   Reading to children and with children

The methods proposed will be within the overall approaches generally in operation in modern infant reception classes. Some of the teaching, for instance, will centre around book time when the teacher will read to the children. There are schools where story reading is done by another adult, and there may be a place for this, but we believe story reading is a skilled job which ought not to be delegated lightly. During this reading the teacher will show the book and print features mentioned above in a natural fashion and without detracting from the enjoyment of the story. However, the teaching will emphasize by drawing the attention of the emergent-reading children in particular to the print features more frequently and directly. The over-riding aspect of the meaningful nature of print, however, will involve all children. These reading sessions are very important for they are also attuning the children to the sounds of language in its written form. The teacher's reading will supply intonation patterns and emphases, that is, be a model of meaningful reading.

It is also pertinent to notice that there is a place for the teacher to read with the individual child. Waterland (1985) has made this practice well known as the apprenticeship approach. It replicates what takes place in the home where some children are read to regularly on a one-to-one basis. Although this is ideal and can be achieved with very small classes, it is virtually impossible on a regular basis with all children in a normal classroom. However, as with other beneficial practices, it is well worth trying to implement as much as possible. The same approach is entailed here. The child is free to choose the book he or she wishes to read and as the teacher reads with the child, she will point out to P1 children the various facets of the book, print and illustrations, allowing the child to read as much as he or she is capable of and taking over the reading when there are unknown words or patterns of language. Some children will not be capable of paired reading even, and the teacher, or other adult, or older child, should read for the child. Some children will pretend to read and in doing so show how far they appreciate the concepts of the book and its print.

(b)   Writing for reading

As well as story time, there is a need for writing time. And here we would point out that writing is probably the best way to learn to read for some of the abstract features about reading are best taught through writing. The concept of print features obviously apply in writing for the child now becomes the author, but there are additional points to be watched. In reading the content is often given, because books are purchased by teachers or headteachers, although practices differ. Children bring their own favourite books to school, sometimes giving them to the school, exchanging them at school and occasionally assisting with the choice. It should be noted that we are talking here of what some call 'real' books, that is books that are not part of a reading scheme. In writing, however, we have to ensure that the child supplies the content. The writer must have something to say and what is to be written by the child must be of interest to the child; it must be about something he or she cares about. In other words it should be as near a real message that someone will read as can be devised. These early messages may be no more than scribbles, but it is surprising how the print or letter features begin to appear. These will receive encouragement as will children's writing of their own names and those of others.

5.   *The evaluation of teaching*

It is always good policy to look back after a period of teaching, say at the half-term break, to evaluate what has been achieved and this should be done alongside the assessment of the children's progress. Obviously you will be aware when you planned to use your chosen methods what you hoped to achieve and now is the time to take stock. Did those methods achieve the results you anticipated? If not, to what extent were they unsuccessful? You will need to consider your informal evaluation of the group's capabilities and whether their needs, as diagnosed, have been met. It is useful to remember that the initial summing up was informal and tentative. Having reviewed your work you can now be more confident that you will be able to plan the next half-term's work more effectively and use the experiences to inform your work with the next group of reception children.

You will also find that some of the work requires more knowledge on your part and you will also need to discuss some of the matters with your colleagues for the school's language policy may need revising.

6.   *The assessment of the children*

Having established the original position of each child on the RDC you will not see how the system will help you account for on going progress. You will need to extend into other positions on the continuum and these are dealt with as we continue through the chapter. We have found that it is useful to prepare a continuum outline for each child and under each position put notes about the child's reading behaviour as observed. Progress can be judged by looking at the movement of that behaviour along the continuum.

Position 2. (P2) Developing reading

In order to continue the assessment of reading we look now at the characteristics of position 2 on the continuum. The main feature of this is the ability of the reader to read groups of words, eventually being able to read and understand complete sentences in familiar settings. You will be able to assess performance again within the reading sessions outlined in P1. By listening carefully for phrasing and fluency you will be able to note where along the continuum the reading is best located. Some will read in small word groupings and these groupings will be linguistically determined. You will be able to use the constituents outlined in Chapter 4 to recognize the progress attained. Some readers will be further along reaching a complete sentence. However, the main determinant of the next position, the perception of cohesion, may not be reached. It is as though more cognitive capacity than is presently available is needed to do this.

Teaching children at Position 2

1. *What needs developing?*
It should be remembered that although children have reached this position and have the strengths of P1 knowledge, their reading is still developing in its fundamentals. To achieve the groupings of words necessary to make sense of the book, a certain amount of automaticity in recognition of words and syntax is needed. Having achieved this, cognitive capacity will be released to deal with processing the larger chunks increasingly involved.

2. *What knowledge is available?*
For the information needed to plan for P2 readers, we refer to three authorities. Firstly to LaBerge and Samuels (1977) whose work on automaticity is pertinent at this point and elsewhere, to Smith (1978) whose insights we have already reported and Morris (1984) who has consistently pointed out the advantages of understanding phonics and linguistic insights.

To some there may appear to be a contradiction in placing the ideas of Smith and Morris together in this section, but there are good reasons to do so. Smith proposes that we learn to read by reading and indeed that is the philosophy that underlies a good deal of the recommendations in P1 teaching; however, he castigates the phonic method of teaching reading. Morris on the other hand in her latest formulations believes that mastery of phonics is a great help towards fluent reading not least because it provides attack skills for unknown words in particular. Her stance receives backing in the Report of the Commission on Reading in the United States, 'Becoming a Nation of Readers', to which we have already referred (Anderson *et al.* 1985).

3. *The teaching strategy*
First there will be a need to continue with the strategy evolved for P1 readers. To this will be added procedures necessary to build the confidence of readers to tackle word groupings and eventually complete sentences.

4. *Some suggested methods*

(a) Reading to children and with children
The methods already used will assist P2 readers as it does those at P1. The

difference being that reading with children will involve leaving longer stretches of language for them to read as they show confidence. Help can be given, not only by reading unknown passages for them, but also beginning to draw attention to the sound associated with the first letter of an unknown word. In this you will keep the meaning in focus but prompt a little by drawing attention to the letter sound association. You will find that children will be aware of these characteristics from their writing where the need to spell often requires some phonic information.

(b)   Writing for reading

Many children write sentences of 'news' for their early writing, and for some this has interest, but if there is no variation it becomes an empty, meaningless task. Many need a more practical or relevant outcome to both motivate and demonstrate the purpose and relevance of writing (Hoffman 1977).

It follows that the language needs to be the child's own and not the teacher's. And here we reach a fundamental problem of how to organize these first writing for reading activities. Probably the most successful method of achieving the theoretical desiderata is the Breakthrough to Literacy method. Many of you will be aware of this but for those who do not, we give a brief description.

The apparatus provided consists of a sentence maker and a number of word banks containing frequently used words that children would need at this stage. The sentence maker is a piece of wood or plastic with a groove down its centre into which children put cards on which words are printed. They select these from the word banks to construct their own sentences. Using this approach, children become used to words being collections of letters separated by spaces, to the concept of a sentence, and some of the conventions of written language like full stops and capital letters. Much is done to ensure that it is the child's own language that is recorded in the sentence maker. The sentence is then copied onto paper and embellished in the usual fashion. There is much to commend this method but, as we will see, it needs up-dating to meet some of the additional knowledge we now have.

(c)   Microcomputer applications

It has been often remarked that one of the major obstacles to progress in writing is the sheer physical difficulty that many children have in manipulating the pencil or other writing implement. Coupled with this is the problem of constructing letters so as to make them recognizable to others and to the child's own satisfaction. It is here that the new technology can be employed to overcome these basic problems. This is not to say that children should not develop a clear handwriting style, but that the composing process should be encouraged to forge ahead unemcumbered in the same way as reading does with most children.

The modern microcomputer is a very versatile machine with a number of very important characteristics, it can spell accurately, its writing is very clear and perfectly formed, it is exceedingly patient and very motivating. Its only drawbacks are that it is expensive, but no more than many pieces of apparatus for which schools raise funds. Secondly, it raises more problems for the teacher than the child. This is because of its technological nature and the adults' knowledge of the early computers that were a mystery to most. However, many teachers have found that their pupils are willing to help them overcome their fears in this regard!

There are now microcomputer programs available that have reproduced the Breakthrough approach for young children. The microcomputer has the Breakthrough word banks stored in its memory and produces the sentence maker feature on the screen. The child only has to recognize the banked words, which are listed at the top of the screen, and press one or two keys to begin composing. The cursor keys can be made to move under the words until the word required is reached. The child then presses the 'copy' key and the word appears in the sentence frame. This procedure is repeated until the sentence is made. The sentence is then printed out to the child's satisfaction. Most authors will be able to read easily what they have written.

There is only room here to sketch the possibilities but the machine's versatility can be utilized in many ways. To begin with, the original card version of the word banks is restricted but the microcomputer has the facility for creating and storing the child's own individual word banks. It also has the great advantage that the contents of the word banks are always available and never get lost, unlike the cards that always need finding, re-sorting, and often replacing. There are also other features that will be outlined later.

5. *The evaluation of teaching*

It is now time to fit the evaluation of your P2 teaching into the cycle begun in P1. You should be looking now at the efficay of the methods you have practised for these children and revise them where necessary or use them for those children moving into this position from P1.

6. *Assessing P2 children*

As with P1, having assessed the children as P2 you will need to place their performance on your individual profile sheets. These will help you to gauge their present strengths and weaknesses as before but within a different continuum position.

As noted earlier it is useful to use the computer storage for these individual profiles.

Position 3. (P3) Extending reading

We reach now an important stage in the reading programme. In order to cater for the children's present cognitive needs and to prepare for later reading demands, it is important, as we have noticed, to introduce into the programme as many non-fiction texts as you have fiction texts. In other words having established sufficient reading skills there is a need to extend reading much further.

Teaching at Position 3

1.   *Assessing the needs*

Some children, even at reception stage, will be showing the characteristics of continuum Position 3. Essentially you will be looking first for the perception of cohesion in texts that are well known. You will be able to detect this quite easily as there are many cohesive ties in all texts. Some of the simplest to assess are the pronouns but you should not rely on these only. They will provide a useful starting point but you should note the examples given in Chapter 2 and look for the reading of those as well. However, you should note now the reader's attempts to replace intonation patterns during oral reading. These may not always be appropriate but nonetheless attempts to impose intonation will appear with the gradual mastery of larger word groupings. During this, if you observe closely, you will find that the cohesive nature of the text assists the phrasing of the reading. If the reader shows this ability but in the process reads sentences inaccurately, then the reading has reached the transition point between P2 and P3. If, in addition, the sentences are read accurately then the child has reached P3.

In order to assess the needs, and recalling the requirement to teach to the next stage, you will want to ensure that cohesion is perceived in a variety of text types. When the text is not fictional or in narrative form you may find that the reading no longer has P3 characteristics thus demonstrating the need for additional help.

2.   *What knowledge is available?*

Here you can be guided by the writing and research about cohesion. You will have noted that cohesive patterns are thought to differ according to author style and register. Other features revealed by the research into children's writing development is the decrease in non-cohesive writing and the increase in cohesive. For example, lack of cohesion was signalled by missing antecedents in pronoun type references. Young authors anticipate that the reader will know to whom the pronoun refers. The writing has the characteristics of speech but the texture of the written word has not developed. Another feature to look for is an increase in lexical cohesion. This is probably related to the development of schemata and their attending language factors. As a schema grows and its internal relationships become established then the vocabulary associated with it will also reflect those relationships. When expressing these concepts this enrichment will be reflected in the writing.

3. The teaching strategy

As well as maintaining the strategies for P1 and P2 children you will need to include those reaching P3 on the continuum. The pupils will already be having factual texts read to them as part of their reading programme, so it is an important step to begin to encourage the reading and writing of non-fiction.

4. Method suggestions

(a) Reading to and with the children

In this you will need to use skilful management techniques, that is, to introduce a variety of texts to children so that they will want to choose and read them. In other words, during the 'free choice' that you will have arranged for the early materials you will expect to see some children choosing factual books to read. In time all must have non-fiction reading experiences. It is not sufficient to leave the introduction of this variation until a later age, say at the junior school, because to become attuned to a variety of genre, children must have early experiences of other texts than the story type. Again this can be achieved during the 'read-with-me' sessions as well as at those times when teacher is reading to the children.

(b) Writing for reading

The same overall conditions apply here as they did in the other positions. However, to meet the writing needs of the P3 children, it is necessary to extend their writing to focus on cohesion. The first development is to increase the capacity of the sentence maker to create a text maker. If you feel apparatus is still necessary, this can be done by providing a simple frame on which to hang the sentences. Then the children can have at least two connected sentences. The word banks need to be checked for cohesive, or connecting words, making sure there is an adequate supply. These can be written on coloured card so that you can more easily encourage children to make sure that there is at least one colourd word present in each sentence. You will no doubt find that there is less and less use made of the apparatus for now the children will be writing more fluently and the apparatus will be discarded.

(c) Microcomputer applications

There are microcomputer programs available that have the Breakthrough approach but that have extended the capacity of the screen to include more than one sentence. In the same way as we have suggested using coloured cards for cohesive words, the word banks can also have the cohesive words in colour. The young authors can have the same rule as those working with cards, that is to have at least one coloured word in each sentence.

(d) Talking about books and authors

While many teachers talk about books during the 'read-with-me' sessions, it is helpful to extend this to involve showing or helping children to discover how authors make meaning. Alongside the writing activities therefore, it is useful to draw attention to the way in which the writers of the books they have been reading achieve cohesion. It is possible to go through a text with a group of children and play 'detectives'. The clues to be followed answer questions of the type, 'How do we know that this is this or that person?' The children can even be asked to follow simple cohesive chains to trace the events of a story. Some children have done this by using coloured pencils to trace the progress of different characters. You will, of course, need to copy parts of a story for this work and should observe any copyright restrictions.

4.   *The evaluation of teaching*

This will be carried out in the same way as noted for the other two positions. You will look back over your previous work considering its effectiveness in the aspects dealt with here. It is unlikely that you will be satisfied with all the elements but you should be able to note those that were successful, those that were not and those that, with modification, would become successful.

Another dimension enters now as you will have been working on activities with P3 children to extend their work at the same time as working with others still at P1 and P2. However, as time goes on those latter children will be working along the continuum to the P3 activities. It is possible, therefore, to modify those activities to ensure greater success for those that are about to reach P3. We have now an evaluation cycle which can become a consistent procedure.

5.   *The assessment of the children*

You will already have made out profile sheets for each child and it will be necessary to assess the position of your P3 children along the continuum. This time, however, you will need to be sure that the assessment includes different types of text. You will now be plotting where the child's reading is in relation to text variety. As indicated, different texts will elicit different performances and your profile for each child will become an informative document showing strengths and weaknesses. From these profiles you will be able to cater for the individual, encouraging those areas of weakness and establishing further the strengths.

Position 4. (P4) Fluent reading

The concept of reading development that we have been discussing is two dimensional. Firstly, there is the reading development that occurs as the child moves from class to class or grade to grade. This movement, in terms of the children's overall growth is both cognitive and linguistic. This is catered for by the programmes of work constructed by the teacher or school for children as they move through the infant school. These programmes, or syllabuses, will be reflected in the choice of activities and books. This dimension can be profiled in addition to the individual profiles. You can construct a class profile and indeed a school profile. The second dimension is the individual's reading development set against the school's requirements. We now reach Position 4 on the RDC for these individual children. To be assessed as being at this position requires reading fluently the whole range of books provided for that age group.

Teaching children at Position 4

1.　*Assessing the needs*

We have already seen how children are spread along the continuum and you will no doubt find that in a short time some are exhibiting reading behaviour on some books, probably fiction, which can be termed fluent. In any case as we are talking about progress throughout the infant school, there will be many able to read, simple texts at least, fluently. By fluently we mean that they are reading the full range of texts with understanding. The problem is to be sure that the text is indeed being read with full understanding. For your teaching you will also need to know the extent of the text linguistic awareness that is supporting that reading.

In the infant school, much of the assessment or judgement of progress is done by hearing children read and indeed we have advocated that method; however, it is easy to be misled be the apparent fluency of the performance. Some other techniques are required, therefore, to assess the on-going needs of these children. One method that has been successfully used, as we saw in the research review, is the deletion procedure. You should note that it is not a random deletion procedure nor a regular cloze procedure, but a technique that involves selecting the author's thread of meaning – the prominent, or main, cohesive chain – and deleting the ends of some of the ties. We proposed earlier that you make a survey of books that are in use in the infant school, and now this survey can be employed. You will have made a selection from your books and will now be able to give children, who in your judgement have reached P4, a number of the related assessment sheets. You should remember to include as many non-fiction as fiction examples. Having asked the children to complete these, each response for each child can be plotted as to its continuum position. From these results you will have a clear picture of the needs of each of the children that have reached P4.

2.　*What knowledge is available?*

Again the work on cohesion, together with the small amount that has been done on register perception, will form the basis of the knowledge base for the children. You will also be able to draw on the vast amount of knowledge that is literary in kind. Unfortunately, it has not been possible to include that in this volume but we hope to do so in the series. You will be guided by the categorization of responses from the OU research examples. You will notice from these that the young reader will bring to the task that register with which they are most familiar. Hence, if they are not attuned to variation then they will bring either the register of speech or the story to the situation. If they do they will not be in the final P4 position. Many however, will be close to that end of the continuum.

3.   The teaching strategy

You will continue to meet the needs of children at an earlier position on the continuum and will also be catering for the needs of those who are more advanced. The overall aim of the strategy is to bring all the children for whom you are responsible to position 4 on all texts. We should emphasize that it is most important to check your survey of the provision of texts very carefully to ensure that there is an adequate variation. Most collections in infant schools appear to have a heavy representation of story or narrative books. Unfortunately, at the time of writing, there is need of a much better supply of books with a factual content.

4.   Example methods

(a)   Reading to and with the children

This will continue as there will be some children that will need the experience and reassurance that it will give. However, for P4 children there will be a need to see the introduction of sustained reading. You will have noted from the surveys in Chapter 4 that there is a great tendency for reading to be restricted to short bursts. It is important to ensure that good habits are started early and every attempt should be made to give children a period of uninterrupted sustained silent reading (USSR) to establish this facet. Remembering the force of the model in literacy development, during this time the teacher should be reading silently her or his own choice of book. It may take time to train children to read their own choice of books silently, but it is significant enough to receive priority.

(b)   Writing for reading

Two elements will come into focus now in the development of children's writing. These are the establishment of cohesion and writing for a variety of audiences. These two together enable children to make use of the textual function of language. This does, understandably, involve considerable thought and preparation.

Firstly, it is of utmost importance that children should want to write. This desire is often best encouraged by the children choosing the writing task themselves. Or, the teacher so arranges the environment and activities that they believe they have chosen the task! The purpose for writing needs to be clear and come from within. A topic for a composition should not be plucked out of the air and given to the children with no other purpose than that their writing is for teacher to read and correct.

Secondly, there is a need to emulate the USSR procedure discussed above, only this time in writing. That is, there should be a time when teacher and children are writing for their own particular purposes.

Thirdly, there is a need for the teacher to so arrange the conduct of writing that it is not thought of as a once and for all exercise. Recently, we have seen the introduction of the notion of conferencing in the teaching of writing (Graves 1983). And the notion that children should be able to draft and re-draft, discussing their writing with the teacher and each other when they feel it is necessary, should be strongly encouraged. During these encounters you will have opportunities to align writing with reading, consistently demonstrating the wholeness of language. It will not have escaped your notice that there is much potential for discussion also in this work.

(c)   Microcomputer applications

When children are at the P4 position the microcomputer will be a most valuable asset. It is possible to introduce children to word processing which makes drafting and redrafting so much easier. Word processing programs are available for this age and children enjoy the mastery over composing that they give them.

Another program that can be used is the type of cohesive tie tracing program designed by Jonathan Anderson. Children using this can have a series of 'in context' cohesive ties to detect and complete. These are useful as through them you can introduce extensions to the work of the children according to where they are along the continuum.

A further benefit that the microcomputer can bring with suitable software is newspaper production, or desk-top publishing as it is sometimes called. We now have many facilities that enable the teacher and children to put together designs, diagrams and print using a variety of different fonts. This is a boom for the imaginative teacher. Furthermore, it is highly motivating for the children, bringing real purposes to their writing. It can be used by children also to print their own books.

You should also be aware of the importance of the microcomputer for assisting you to manage the profile system and, as we will see, the class and school records.

(d)   Talking about books and authors

We have spoken very briefly of the importance of creating a literary background alongside the other features mentioned. And here you should not neglect to discuss the characteristics of factual writing with children as well as the craft of the story teller. The latter is often done in schools by invitations to well-known authors to visit and talk with the children, but you rarely find an invitation to others to show how writing plays an important role in their work.

For example, the local policeman is asked into school for many purposes and children might be intrigued to know what goes in that little black book and how his writing might be used in court. The caution, 'And anything you say may be taken down and used in evidence!' might bring a more sophisticated class discussion than many others.

5.   The evaluation of teaching

By this time, having already established your evaluation cycle, you will be able to take a more inclusive appraisal of the teaching that you have been doing with your particular group over a longer period of time, say a year. This will now enable you to combine with your colleagues to obtain an overview of the work of the school by bringing together all the profiles. This is made possible by the conception of the RDC for, from the first, the continuum has been a vehicle by which you and your colleagues can assess the child, the group, the class and together the school. You will now have a basis for discussion to improve the achievements of the school and hence the children attending the school. The class profiles will provide the type of documentation necessary for the Headteacher to present in reports to the School Governors and, if called upon, for teacher appraisal. They will also be acceptable on all sides as teachers have originated them. All this documentation can be economically stored in a microcomputer and produced in different formats.

6.   The assessment of the children

It is part of the cycle to include the results of the deletion tasks that were mentioned above. The resulting profile will contain substantial information that can be discussed with the individual child. This is preferable to the race to get onto the next book in the scheme. The profiles will also have been of benefit as individual records on which the class and school records are based. They will be invaluable to the child's next class or grade teacher as well as being a standard document from which to report to and discuss progress with parents.

Review

In this chapter we have attempted to apply the research on cohesion and register that led to the concept of a reading development continuum. This, and the implementation of the profiling system, has provided a framework for the teaching of reading in the infant school. The chapter included suggested methods for teaching and evaluation.

CHAPTER 7

Teaching reading in the junior school

Introduction

It is assumed that the teacher in the junior school will have read the previous chapter, if not in detail at least in outline. It would help if this has been done, for the format for this chapter assumes the detail of that chapter. Further, although there were factors in the previous chapter that are more directly pertinent to the infant school, some of the features are applicable throughout schooling: we go on to review these first.
review these first.

We have learned that language is a social semiotic system, a system of signs. It is basically this system and its ramifications that junior children are learning to use to make meaning and to recover meaning. We have observed also that there are some recently proposed extensions to the most frequently quoted linguistic descriptions, that is cohesion and register. These, together with the other moves in the study of reading, have required us to rethink the reading process as it pertains to today's schools. And here you should remember that to be literate involves not only being able to read and write but to begin to use these skills to create new literate materials and new understandings (Cook-Gumperz 1986).

School-parent relationships

It is perhaps a strange phenomenon that, after the child has begun to settle into school life, the interest of many parents beings to wane. It is possible, being aware that this is often the case, to counteract any such decline in support by building into school policy ways of maintaining, and if necessary, reviving interest. In the same way as we advised infant teachers, we see the continuance of healthy parent/school relationships as a necessity. If your school is combined junior and infant school then you could be forgiven for thinking that it is only a matter of continuing with the policies begun earlier.

This could be dangerous for, unless you have been directly involved at an early stage and have got to know the parents when the children first started school, you may find problems in establishing the desired relationships. This is because with many parents, mostly mothers, there is a shared knowledge with school staff in terms of caring for young children. As the child grows the knowledge required becomes more education centred and some parents begin to feel out of their depth and, in a way, threatened. To be fruitful and to keep interest high all teachers need to be actively involved from the start. If you teach in a separate junior school, it is quite possible to continue, or begin, a dialogue. In this the guidelines given to the infant teachers need observing. You will need to become aware, for example, of the outside activities of your children at their present age level. Are they in the scout or guide movement? Are they members of the local library? Are they often taken on visits by their parents to other geographical areas? Have they older or younger brothers and sisters in the school? Have they a collection of books? And have they a home computer? All this information will enable you to plan activities to maintain the progress made in the infant school and to close up the 'gap' mentioned by Donaldson, for now it may be widening despite the best endeavours of all concerned.

Some of you may have read about the importance of the home background in a recent study of the achievement of children in science at school. Carried out by Wendy Keys for the National Foundation for Educational Research, the study showed that the single most important factor (Keys, 1987) was the socio-economic level of the parents. This was measured by parents' jobs, level of education, choice of daily newspaper, the approximate number of books in the home and whether there was a computer. This home influence accounted for 23 per cent of the difference in achievement, whereas the type of school accounted for only 0.5 per cent. Although there are many more details in the report and it was concerned with science education only, there can be little doubt of the continuing strong effects of the home on some children's education. Of course, the school cannot make up for all these factors; however, the research into literacy development indicates that active parent-teacher cooperation enhanges this aspect of children's education. And note, this research has been carried out mostly at the junior school level. We repeat, parents have one great advantage over the teacher: they can usually arrange for a one to one situation on a regular daily basis to give practice in reading and writing. Furthermore, the very fact that they are cooperating gives the school added backing and demonstrates to the child that they value what the teacher values. While many teachers aim at individual teaching there is nothing to replace the benefits that true parent cooperation can contribute to this aspect.

A teaching programme outline

in the previous chapter, the structure of the proposed programmes are in form of answers to six basic interrelated questions:

1. What aspects of literacy needs developing?
2. What knowledge is now available to help?
3. What teaching strategies can be designed to meet the needs?
4. What teaching methods are required?
5. How might the teaching be evaluated?
6. How might the pupils be evaluated?

The suggested programmes that follow attempt to answer these questions for the range of abilities that will face the teacher.

The junior years

Assessing the needs

The RDC takes reading to be on a continuum or cline, that is, it is a continuity of development. For the purpose of diagnosing the needs of each child we consider this development in terms of the range of texts chosen for your age group and falling within four continuum positions. As we have seen, this increasing skill (emergent-reading, that is, before the child has demonstrated the ability to read a few words, developing reading, extending reading, fluent reading) is applied to the range of curriculum texts. We begin then to apply the principles of the continuum to reading in the junior school.

In order to do this, all continuum positions will be taken together for three reasons. Firstly, we have already spelt out how the approach to structuring your teaching position by position works out in Chapter 6. Secondly, in the junior school, as in the infant school, teaching is usually in mixed ability groups where children display the characteristics of all the continuum positions. And thirdly, it is now important to interrelate the activities. It also has the advantage of being more economical in presentation and your reading time!

As the reading becomes more learning oriented it will be necessary to ensure that children leave the junior school with the requisite study skills to enable them to succeed at the secondary stage. These features are mentioned below.

All RDC positions

It should be pointed out that although the tasks that follow should be as accurately assessed as possible, it is intended that they should be carried out in normal classroom conditions and built into the day to day activities of the group. On no account should they acquire a test type aura, because children need to develop, if they have already done so, a love of book and such 'testing', if oppressive, could be counter productive.

The first task consists of checking each child's level of literacy. If the profiles have been passed on to you from the infant school your task will be made easier; however, you must now use the range of materials that will be read by your age group as the basis for your own profiles. By now the range of reading ability, P1 to P4, within the class will have extended towards the P3 and P4 positions. Only a few will need their reading checking by oral methods. If there is such a need then you should read that part of Chapter 6 that deals with this in detail. For the majority you will be able to use the cohesive tie deletion procedure on your own range of books. This should be set up as illustrated in Chapter 5.

Teaching children at the four continuum positions

1.   What knowledge is available?

There is a considerable bank of knowledge for junior teachers contained within the three major reading projects surveyed in Chapter 4. There you will find advice on the extension of reading in the junior school provided by the research team based at Manchester University. The team's findings apply directly to the junior age range. And here the work proposed on developing the 'listening to individuals read' is particulary pertinent to P1 and indeed all children. Further, the work from the Nottingham project produced information about the final year of the junior school, and this was complemented and extended by the research carried out at the Open University into cohesion and genre.

You may need to obtain copies of the Manchester and Nottingham reports for more detail than we have been able to give in our very brief summaries.

2.   The teaching strategy

As we have mentioned earlier the continuum stretches from the absence of formal reading skill to the ability to read a great variety of texts fluently. As we continue to foster literacy development we need to build on the work already done in the infant school and at home and so extend reading and writing. Much of the work will be moving from learning to read to reading to learn. While children are learning to read they are, of course learning; however, there will be a greater emphasis on the acquisition of knowledge for a whole variety of curriculum purposes. If the foundations have been laid firmly. earlier it will be very much a process of maintaining progress as the work is extended to cover new texts at varying levels of difficulty. Also involved will be the encouragement of individual independent learning from texts. To make the best of the printed word it will be necessary to teach some basic study skills during this time.

The strategies proposed involve two pairs of basic principles that will guide you as you promote literacy in the junior school. These are the need to ntinue to develop the love of books and reading. And although this involves all types of books many, who are deeply committed to this aspect of reading, usually have fiction or novels in mind. However, to raise the awareness of all concerned we note again the importance of the reading of factual material in a balanced reading diet.

The other pairs of principles, while related to the above, concern those technical aspects of texts, that is cohesion and genre. These provide much needed guidance to both content and methods.

Some teachers may prefer a more direct strategy with any one group of readers at any continuum position or mixture of positions. A strategy known as the Directed Reading Lesson (Binkley 1986) can be followed. This format has three stages, preparation, reading and discussion. It is suggested that the first stage is often missed and the children go straight into the reading followed by discussion. It is suggested that this is an ineffective way of working.

3. The methods

(a) *Reading to children and with children*

The overall approach will be within those methods generally in operation in the modern junior school. However, there is a noticeable tendency not to read to children in the junior school as much as is done in the infant school and this puts children at a great disadvantage. You should, therefore, continue a programme of reading to and with children. First, reading *to* them to attune them to different text types and secondly, to read *with* them, perhaps in small groups, to share books with them.

One of the techniques advocated to help individual children read is paired reading (Morgan 1986) Over the last 10 years or so this has become an important technique for parents to use with their children at home. It also finds its place in school for the pairing can be between one child and another, or teacher and child, or parent, or other, adult and child. It is furthermore a common sense approach which fits easily into the procedures advocated earlier.

(b) *Discussion*

During these sessions there will be that kind of informal discussion about a book that is so valuable and which is applicable to all RDC positions. It will be a simple move to introduce children to discussion techniques at the early junior stage. They may, of course, already be used to the process in the infant school. These techniques will become more important, however, as the children move through the junior age range. Indeed one of the basic methods will be groups of children working together discussing and teasing out a text's meanings. In this, we do not see those children needing particular assistance, being isolated in any way from the rest. However, individual needs do need meeting during mixed ability teaching and the profiles will help you to monitor this.

(c) Vocabulary

An area that will need extending is vocabulary. In this we consider, if we have interpreted the research correctly, the building up of background knowledge prior to reading as being an important factor. Langer (1981) proposed a method of determining and extending the level of prior knowledge of a group of children by a Pre-reading plan (PReP) for assisting understanding. To begin with, the teacher must select a key concept from the topic or text to stimulate discussion. Th PReP then consists of three phases:

1. Tell me anything that comes to mind when...
2. What made you think of ...
3. Based on our discussion, have you any new ideas about...

The first phase is one of free association when the combined knowledge of the group will be explored. The next phase helps the pupils to discover how they arrived at the knowledge they have contributed. At the same time they are learning from the ideas of the rest of the group and perhaps changing their ideas as they interact. In the third phase the children are able to put their notions into words and it has been found that they now become more precise.

Summarizing this procedure Langer states:

> Through the PReP, teachers are helped: 1) to determine the levels of concept sophistication of the individuals in the group; 2) to become aware of the language the students have used to express their knowledge about the subject: and 3) to make judgments about how much more background information students need before reading a text.

We saw earlier in Chapter 4 that the level of children's vocabulary was one of the telling features of the OU research. The extent of the range of vocabulary available in any one group of children was considerable. The clusters were seen to have a structure like a semantic field, that is there was a central core of words that were close synonyms and surrounding this the field dispersed with meanings becoming more and more distant from that of the core. The words at the periphery of the field sometimes reflected the particular interests of the children with only the most tenuous and vague connections with the core. It was as though the associations were drawn from vocabulary knowledge further and further away from the central meaning of the schema evoked by the passage. It was obvious, as we observed, that some children, those in positions 1 and 2 on the continuum, had only a vague idea of the text's overall message. It is quite clear that the background knowledge of children needs building so as to extend their comprehension, perhaps in the way suggested by Langer.

A further practical guide is given by Marzano (1984), who has provided a list of what he called superclusters which are intended for classroom teachers to help structure their vocabulary instruction. Examples of superclusters are:

> Types of motion: action, stillness, begin, end, chase, toss, pull, plunge, shrink.
>
> Time (names of various points and periods of time and words indicating various time

relationships between ideas): lifetimes, noon, season, month, today, earlier, now, afterwards.

These clusters were not just thought up by Marzano but were trawled from a series of sources like books of word frequency lists as well as a book on Basic Elementary Reading Vocabulary. The resulting collection was then organized into 61 clusters by Marzano and reviewed by teachers iteratively until the content of most of the clusters was agreed. It is suggested that the clusters are used to show children the company any particular new, or unfamiliar word, keeps. Many of you may not need this type of resource but for those who are unsure it does give an idea of how vocabulary associations may be grouped in memory. Of course, the schema or concept will not be only in terms of words and their associations, it will contain such things as knowledge of behaviour and other factors concerned with any particular concept.

(d) Directed reading activities

The research team at Nottingham University produced a series of directed reading activities as a result of their work. These DARTS (cf. Binkley 1986 above) as they are called are a basis for the work on texts that we have been working towards. There are five kinds of reading activities suggested by the team. These five, which we mention briefly, are:

1. group cloze.
2. group SQ3R.
3. group sequencing.
4. group prediction.
5. group reading for different purposes (Lunzer and Gardiner 1979:308)

You need to be fully aware that the grouping of children for these purposes is not by age or ability but for the learning from texts that is envisaged. The groups may, therefore, contain children at any continuum position.

All the group study the same material individually and each pupil brings his or her own experiences to it. The group work, because each contributes to the whole, is motivating and children learn to defend their point of view.

One point that needs emphasizing, and one missed by many, is the role of the teacher in this work. As it is most desirable to involve the children to develop the skills of argument and conviction in their opinions, they must not be stifled. However, the teacher should not just leave them to it. The teacher knows the content, the students and the desired effect.

1.   Group cloze

Many of you will now be familiar with cloze procedure and its benefits when used as the basis for group discussion. The rationale behind the procedure was discussed in Chapman (1983) and is at the heart of the Nottingham proposals referred to here. One version of the procedure involves making deletions at set intervals, say every seven words, and then asking children to replace the words individually. The children then come together into their group to discuss their choice of words. The resulting discussion has been found to be an effective learning experience.

Another version of the deletion procedure is the one used in the OU research. This is to identify the cohesive chain and then to make deletions of the end of a number of ties. This has been found to call for a greater in-depth understanding of the text.

You will have noticed that there are ample opportunities to follow the strategies mentioned earlier in these procedures. This particularly applies to genre and register.

2.   Group SQ3R

In this children first make a quick survey of the text (S) taking in such things as title, layout and subheadings. As they do this they raise questions (Q) as a result of their survey. During this operation the group will discuss the questions and the text. Next the text is read through (R1) and then reviewed (R2). As this is done, salient points are identified and discussed and finally recited (R3). Here the outcome is essentially the recall of the salient points.

3.   Group sequencing

This activity involves the preparation of several sections of a story, poem, set of instructions, expository or other type of text. Children work in pairs on this material with the aim of putting the sections in an order to makes sense. You will be aware that there are many ways of arranging the sections so that they are more or less demanding.

4.   Group prediction

In this an instalment from a passage is distributed to the group and the children are required to predict what happens next. It is suggested that this activity has a chairman, the teacher, who will summarize the discussion. The instalments are then collected in to prevent referral back. The team point out that a story with an unexpected, though plausible, ending encourages a lively debate.

These activities are mentioned only briefly here and you are advised to read the original sources for more detail.

(e)   Study skills

Many of the above suggestions come under the teaching of study and skills and need attention during the junior years to establish efficient study habits. These will be included in your early evaluation of the needs of the class.

To help you organize this area is a very useful book prepared by Graham and Robinson (1984). The contents of this book are organized in three stages and the chapter headings for these give you an indication of their organization:

1.   Before the eyes meet the page,
2.   While the eyes are on the page, and
3.   After the eyes leave the page.

In the first of these, setting the purpose of the reading session should be decided at the outset. So, if your class is embarking on a central topic of study, some discussion of the reasons for the activity and the part to be played by each student needs organizing. Sarah Tann has drawn attention to the mismatch of the perceptions of teachers and children as to the purpose of topic work in schools (Tann 1987). Although her sample of teachers and children was small her findings give us cause to ponder when she states:

> Topic work appears to be viewed in a very limited fashion. It is about finding things out. It is book based. It provides opportunities for children to pick up study skills. It results in lots of writing for the children. Few records are kept. There is little in the way of systematic planning or the progression of skills, attitudes, knowledge or concepts throughout a child's school experience. There is little awareness amongst the children of what they are learning and there is little attempt by the teachers to analyse the potential and to identify what the children might be learning. Having developed a way of doing Topic work teachers then tend to stick with it. The children soon learn the knack of getting by. No wonder some of the children come to feel that it is boring and samey. However, this was also the feeling of many of the teachers! Many of them were dissatisfied and looking for change.

It is with this situation in mind, and we do have to recall that the sample may have been less than representative, that we propose the type of overall planning suggested here. In this more systematic way some of the lack of direction indicated in the quote may be avoided. But there is another important facet to this study skill area 'while the eyes are on the page'.

An important part of the organization of the material in a book is conveyed by the various lay-out features. There are many of these modern educational books and it is wise to check that they are there when you are purchasing new books. There should be 'a table of contents', 'a statement of the book's purpose as an information text', 'advanced organizers', 'clear chapter headings and sub-headings', 'adequate summaries', and 'a comprehensive index'. To these will be added some of the following according to the book's purpose and content: pictures, diagrams, maps, graphs, tables, glossary, bibliography, notes, guide questions, review questions and other types of typographical aids. Your students will need to be acquainted with the purpose of each of these as they move through the junior school. They will also require practice, *by use in real research*.

In time, however, your pupils will begin to suggest their own purposes for reading. But they will continue to need some type of PReP activity to introduce the topic and other experiences, both direct and contrived, in anticipation of the study. They will need to be familiar with ways of interacting with the text, for example, by the DARTS activities outline above. We need to be sure that the discipline of efficient study is laid down before the children leave the junior school.

After reading, there is the third stage which is called postorganizing activities by Graham and Robinson. In this they list retention of what has been learned, report writing and test taking.

As you begin to introduce the notion of systematic methods of study, you should bear in mind that your aim is to gradually withdraw from actually teaching the skills. In other words, as time passes the children should develop good study skills as a matter of habit. Your only task then, will be to monitor or check that they continue to read effectively and efficiently.

(f)   Writing

We would reiterate here that writing is probably the best way to learn about some of the subtle characteristics of reading (Stewart-Dore 1986). For some of these abstract features can be made more visible during the teaching of writing. Again, as we pointed out before, the writer must have something to say and what is to be written by the child must be of interest to the child; it must be about something he or she really cares about. In other words it should be as near a real message that someone will read as can be devised. In this it is crucial that they feel the pull of an audience and it is in this that teachers will need as much ingenuity as they can muster. As we have noted before many need a more practical or relevant outcome to both motivate and demonstrate the purpose and relevance of writing (Hoffman 1977).

It is anticipated that during the junior school there will be considerable development of writing. One of the main features will be the ability to write for different audiences. A very useful book for this is Kress (1982) who traces the ability of children to write in different styles and genres. He also shows how great are the differences between speech and writings as well as dealing with other factors in the writing process. We give some ideas for starting different kinds of writing in Appendix 6. It will be helpful if the teacher can draw together the various language strands for the children when writing is taking place. Work will have been done in drama and puppetry for example, where the appropriateness of the language used by the characters can be commented on. This language awareness is of obvious importance but it may not carry over to writing. Similarly with reading, where the links can be made during the discussion of texts as mentioned above. In addition, a more individual approach can be made during the writing conferences with the teacher. In all this work writing should be seen to develop by the child. They should feel and know that they are making progress to becoming an author.

Microcomputer applications

It is envisaged that the microcomputer will have become familiar to all children and that some of its potential already realized. What is certain is that it has applications across the whole range of abilities and curriculum offerings. In this we need to mention that, wherever possible, the various topics usually found in the junior school curriculum should not be isolated from each other. This is particularly important when the microcomputer is involved. All the while it is being used there is a 'reading lesson' being undertaken.

In an interesting paper (Anderson 1984), we learned that there were three ways of using the microcomputer in schools. These were its use as a tutor, tutee, and tool in language and reading activities. Most will recognize its possibilities as an instructional device and as a tool. However, although it has been called an 'imagination machine' it is rare to find it being taught. We mention this because it is not always used creatively, that is by teaching children computer programming, and it is this aspect that needs to be explored further. In the following we see most of the roles identified by Anderson.

We have outlined the use of deletion type tasks as the basis for encouraging children to interrogate texts. There are useful computer programs available that create the cloze texts for you. One such, Gap maker...Gap taker, is an ingenious programme which provides cloze type activities on the screen using its own sample texts. It also provides the facility for the creation of your own texts which can be stored on separate discs. The program enables you to 'Make' or change a story, 'Take' or read a story, add or change deletions and conceal or reveal the words deleted. It is also possible, as you will have realized, for children to create their own stories and set deletion tasks for you or other children.

Another program from the same author, Jonathan Anderson, is 'Tie tracer'. This program is a general purpose tool that may be used with any classroom material. It has been tested on children across the primary and secondary age ranges, and with children with special needs. One of the uses that is pertinent here is tracing the threads of meaning that tie a text together.

The program has a simple introductory passage which helps to establish the routines. Take the demonstration story 'Foster' for example:

Dr Foster went to Gloucester
in a shower of rain
.. stepped in a puddle
right up to his middle
And he never went .. again

The user moves the cursor key until it is under the blank and then types in whatever word he or she thinks best. The text will accommodate different lengths of words. When finished children can press the 'copy' key and compare their words with the words deleted.

This is only one way in which the program can be used; the program has a greater potential than this. Anderson tells us about it as follows:

Some of the specific aims of Tie Tracer are to provide students, at all levels of reading ability, with:
1. some insight into the properties of text and so improve their comprehension;
2. practice of reading a wide variety of texts in the context of a whole language approach;
3. an appreciation of register so that they are able to distinguish between what is appropriate and what is inappropriate in particular writing situations:
4. an understanding of the way language functions in written text; and
5; the opportunity to develop their reading and writing vocabularies.

In so far as the program is used by students in groups, it also promotes discussion about language.

You will appreciate that these types of programs go a long way to providing activities that are in line with the theoretical stance we have taken as a result of the OU research.

Again, although there is only room to sketch in possibilities for reading and writing, it is hoped the suggestions will act as leads into other activities.

4. The evaluation of teaching

As we mentioned in the previous chapter it is always good policy from a professional point of view to look back after a period of teaching, say at the half-term break, to evaluate what has been achieved and this should be done alongside the assessment of the children's progress. In addition there is now some considerable pressure being put on teachers to become accountable to their employers, parents and governing bodies. As we discussed in Chapter 6, you will be aware when you planned to use your chosen strategies and methods what you hoped to achieve. Now is the time to take stock. Did those methods achieve the result you anticipated? If not, to what extent were they unsuccessful? You will need to consider your evaluation of the group's capabilities and whether their needs, as diagnosed, have been met.

You will also find that some of the work requires more knowledge on your part and you will need to read further the references given at various points in this volume. There will also be further books in this series that will explore some of the issues at a greater depth. You will also need to discuss some of the matters with your colleagues for the school's language policy may well need revising to encompass the rethinking you are doing.

5. The assessment of the children

In whatever way was appropriate you will have established the original position of each child on the RDC. By re-assessing at various times, say at half and full-term breaks, you will see how the profiling system will help you account for on-going progress. We assume that you will have prepared a continuum outline for each child and under each position put notes about the child's reading behaviour and attitudes to reading (and writing) as it is observed. Progress can be judged by looking at the movement of that behaviour along the continuum.

There is a further dimension that can be explored. The system, as we saw in Chapter 4, allows the creation of group and class profiles by amalgamating the individual profiles. These are useful documents as they enable you to demonstrate the progress of the whole school plotted year by year: a valuable demonstration for any head to take to a governing body. The advantages is that the profile is built from the curriculum of the school. It is not an arbitrary device controlled by statistics and imposed from outside the school.

Review

As with the previous chapter, we have attempted to provide a structure for your work with proposals for classroom activities based on research, together with a management technique. Using a wholistic approach to language work, we have emphasized the need to extend the reading curriculum so as to embrace a wide variety of text types.

CHAPTER 8

Conspectus

It is now 10 years since the writer presented a paper at 'The Processing of Visible Language Conference' held in 1977 at Eindhoven, Holland on the 'Perception of language cohesion during fluent reading' (Chapman 1979a). In 1978, a paper entitled 'Pedagogical strategies for fluent reading' (Chapman 1979b), was read to the 15th Annual Course and Conference of the United Kingdom Reading Association. This paper introduced the cohesion proposals to reading teachers for the first time. These have become two quests, for the place of cohesion in the fluent reading process and the development of its use in pedagogical strategies. They have been followed constantly during the intervening years. During this time, as we have seen, there have been considerable movements in thinking about reading, its acquisition and teaching.

We have covered a considerable number of topics in this swift review of these developments in reading, and we need now to gather some of the threads together. We begin with one of the criticisms we mentioned earlier, for this helps to clarify the topic and as it has had a greater effect on research than it deserves, it needs comment.

Cohesion, as defined by Halliday and Hasan (1976, 1980) is, in essence, a global concept of texts with local implications. It is one of the characteristics of text being a sub-component of the text-forming component of the semantic system. Further, as its parentage is in Halliday's linguistics it resides within a social semiotic perspective of language and is, thereby, closely associated with another concept, that of register. If you examine the diagram of the functions of language Halliday (1973:141) you will note that cohesion occupies a small section only at the textual end of the chart. Again, in the latest volume on functional grammar, Halliday (1985), it is one chapter out of 10. It is, then, not an isolated concept but part of one particular description of language. We cannot isolate cohesion in the way so many do when applying it in research studies.

The definition of linguistics employed by Morgan and Sellner (1980) in their critique of the cohesion proposals, for example does not apply to the linguistic parentage of cohesion. The findings arising out of mismatch are thereby less creditable than they might have been. In particular, the concept of register must be assigned an important role, for it cannot be lightly dismissed. However, if a positive stance is taken to the work and its perspective, then we find the proposals are in line with modern trends in thinking about literacy education and lead directly to many classroom and school applications.

We noted in the first chapter that the view of reading being primarily a language process has gained greater recognition recently in the study of reading. In addition the wholistic nature of language has come to the fore with such concepts as emerging literacy. Alongside these features there has been a noticeable interest in the 'tutoring' potential of parents both directly and indirectly before formal schooling and directly in cooperation with teachers when the child is at school. These developments have taken place in a changing world scene where the nature of our culture has become increasingly technical and competitive. Whatever point of view is taken about the debate on reading standards there are signs that there is a need for teachers to rethink their views on reading so as to meet the challenges.

In the next two chapters we first reviewed some of the work of Halliday and his colleagues, for if reading is to be fully conceived as a language process then there is need of a unified theory on which to base it. There are many theories of language, each having their strengths and weaknesses; however, in our opinion only this one meets the various demands made by education.

This very brief and incomplete introduction to Halliday's work was followed by a review of thinking about reading in this and other countries. We noted the contrast in the pronouncements made about our knowledge of reading in this country with the more optimistic outlook in the United States of America. Research there has gone ahead with vigour, and advances in understanding of the reading process are claimed.

In Chapter 3 we gathered together some of the reading research that has been carried out, such as that concerned with schemata, metacognition and text structure. These are still being explored, and the concept of schemata and its place in the reading process has been extended recently by Hirsch (1987) and incorporated within a notion of cultural literacy. In this we find the type of knowledge we used to call common knowledge. The book gives lists of (American) words and concepts the author suggests as being needed to survive in today's culture.

We also collected together some of the research that has been done following the publication of Halliday and Hasan's analysis of cohesion. Using this basis these research studies investigated the place of cohesion in reading and writing. Only a few of the studies carried out were quoted; the selection being based on adherence to Halliday and Hasan's description and their classroom relevance. It is interesting to note in passing how some investigations have added or subtracted certain elements (e.g. Freebody and Anderson 1983), and how some have made assumptions of their own (Mosenthal and Tierney 1981) or accepted without question the critique of Morgan and Sellner. While it is possible to find lack of rigour in some of the studies we have quoted, they do retain the original description of cohesion, making it possible to compare and contrast findings, and have the teaching situation as their focus.

From these studies it is possible to discern the early beginnings of a development in thought regarding the influence of texture on reading. This concerns the move from simply counting the number of cohesive ties and trying to ascertain if certain groups of ties make comprehension more or less difficult, to a greater concern with the integration of meaning during the reading of a complete text. The notion of the chaining of cohesive ties, though apparent in the 1976 publication, was not taken up until after the treatment given to the topic in Halliday and Hasan (1980). Following the visit made by Halliday and Hasan to the OU project, chaining was considered to be most important in the research team's preparation of the materials for their survey of reading development. In this, as we have noted, the classroom relevance of educational research was emphasized.

One further useful conribution made by the studies quoted lies in the variety of methods used. This gives some stability to the concept's reality in reading processing for the findings are mostly positive.

In Chapter 4, the school based reading research carried out at Nottingham and Manchester Universities was reviewed while that at the Open University was presented in more detail. Some of the findings of the latter project were interpreted as follows:

1. The ability of children to perceive cohesive relationships in their school texts was pertinent to reading development in schools.
2. The perception of register, as the realization of genre, has to be considered alongside of the perception of cohesion.
3. It is possible, using these two concepts along with other insights from systemic linguistics, to create profiling systems for school, class and individual.
4. Using the concepts of cohesion and register, there are clear indications that children, whose reading performance on standardized reading tests is advanced, provide more accurate reflections of the author's textual meaning than those whose performance is average or below the average of the age group.
5. There is clear evidence of a lack of reading progress of the lower band of readers (i.e. the lowest third scorers on the standardized reading test). This was found to be particularly serious in the secondary schools.

This research collected a great deal of data, the majority of which concerns secondary reading. These findings will be given in a further volume on the teaching of reading in the secondary school.

In this volume, after presenting the data of the survey, we began a presentation of proposals for incorporating the finding of the OU and other research into classroom practice. This we did within a management system which involved both teacher and child evaluation. The proposals are meant to be broad enough for you to develop your own programme of teaching within their confines. We hope you will find them useful.

Appendix 1

Lists of books (with publisher's permission to use for research purposes) from
which excerpts were drawn

Junior books

R. Dahl, *Charlie and the Chocolate Factory*, George Allen & Unwin Ltd., 1964; M. Sendak,
The Sign on Rosie's Door, The Bodley Head, 1969; D. Edwards, *When My Naughty Little
Sister Was Good*, Methuen Children's Books Ltd., 1957; C.S. Lewis, *The Lion the Witch and
the Wardrobe*, Collins Publishers, 1950; J.G. Robinson, *More About Teddy Robinson*, George
Harrap, 1959; A.E. Tansley, *Sound Sense* Book 3B, E.J. Arnold & Son Ltd., 1974; T.
Clymer, *We like to Laugh*, Reading 360, Level 6, Book 4, illustrate by V.W. Jones, Ginn &
Co Ltd., 1978; P. Lippman, *Busy Wheels*, Random House Inc., N.Y., 1973; F.J. Schonell
& P. Flowerdew, *Wide Range Readers* Green Book 1, Oliver & Boyd, 1950; Gray, Munroe,
Artley & Arbuthnot, *Here and There: The Good Story Readers*, A. Wheaton & Co Ltd., 1956;
Brer Rabbit Stories, BBC Publications, 1968; C. Storr, *Puss and Cat*, Faber and Faber Ltd.,
1969. Reprinted by permission of the publishers; M. Osborne, *The Horro billy Goes to
School*, illustrated by E. Browne, Heinemann Easy to Read, 1979; N. Hunter, *The Peculiar
Triumph of Professor Branestawm*, The Bodley Head, 1970. L. Ingalls Wilder, *Little House in
the Big Woods*, Methuen Children's Books Ltd., 1932. R. Kerrond, *A First Look at Weather*,
Franklin Watts, Ltd., 1972; J. Bendick, *The Future Explorers' Club Meets Here*, Ginn 360,
Level 9, Book 4, Ginn & Co. Ltd., 1978; *Time to Wonder*, Ginn 360, Level 8, Book 5, Ginn
& Co Ltd., 1978; S. Paulson Russel, *Through a Magic Glass*, Ginn 360, Level 8, Book 5,
Ginn & Co Ltd., 1978; H. Adams, *Policemen and the Police Force*, Basil Blackwell, 1962; L.G.
Humphrys, *Drinks*, Basil Blackwell, 1971; J. Leigh-Pemberton, *Baby Animals*, published by
Ladybird Books Ltd., Loughborough, 1974. Reproduced by permission of the publishers;
Spiders, Macdonald First Library, 1971. Copyright © Macdonald Educational Limited;
Rocks and Mining, Macdonald First Library, 1971. Copyright © Macdonald Educational
Limited; Howell, Walker & Fletcher, *Mathematics for Schools*, Book 2, Level II, Addison
Wesley, London, 2nd edn. 1980; 'Track Down Early Railways', from the *Science Museum
Quiz Guide for Young Visitors*, 1978; E.J. Schonell & P. Flowerdew, 'The Story of Light',
Wide Range Readers, Green Book 6, Oliver & Boyd, 1953; Evertts, Van Roekel & Murray,
Seven Seas Nisbet & Co Ltd., 1975; Althea, *Bridges*, Dinosaur Publications Ltd., 1973; G.
Carsdale, *Learnabout Pets*, published by Ladybird Books Ltd., Loughborough, '1977.
Reproduced by permission of the publishers; A. Darlington, *Experiments with your
Microscope*, Carousel Books Ltd., 1977. Reproduced by permission of Transworld
Publishers, London; J. Webster, *Man and his Car* published by Ladybird Books Ltd.,
Loughborough, 1974. Reproduced by permission of the publishers: E. Holt, *Cats*,
Copyright © Franklin Watts Ltd., 1973.

Secondary books

I. Serrailier, *The Silver Sword,* Jonathan Cape Ltd., 1954; W. Golding, *Lord of the Flies,* Faber & Faber Ltd., 1954. Reprinted by permission of the publishers; L. Ingalls Wilder, *Little House in the Big Woods,* Methuen Children's Books Ltd., 1932; B. Glanville, *Goalkeepers are Different,* Hamish Hamilton, 1971. Reprinted by permission of John Farquharson, Authors Agent; R. Lancelyn Green, *King Arthur and His Knights of the Round Table,* pp.120–123, Penguin Books Ltd., 1953. Reprinted by permission of the publishers; N. Hunter, *The Peculiar Triumph of Professor Branestawm,* The Bodley Head, 1970; R. Sutcliff, *The Lantern Bearers,* Oxford University Press, 1959; R. Dahl, *Danny the Champion of the World,* Jonathan Cape Ltd., 1977; U. Le Guin, *Wizard of Earthsea,* Victor Gollancz Ltd., 1968; G. Kemp, *The Turbulent Term of Tyke Tiler,* Faber & Faber Ltd., 1977. Reprinted by permission of the publisher; C. Dickens, *David Copperfield,* Oxford Illustrated Dickens, Oxford University Press, 1948. G. Carsdale, *Learnabout Pets,* published by Ladybird Books Ltd., Loughborough, 1977. Reproduced by permission of the publishers; A. Darlington, *Experiments with your Microscope,* Carousel Books Ltd., 1977. Reproduced by permission of Transworld Publishers, London; B. Bailey & E. Wise, *Focus on History: The Early Stuarts,* Longman Group Ltd., 1971. Drakett, *Let's Look at Motor Cars,* Frederick Muller Ltd., J. & D. Ashby, *Looking at the World Today,* Adam & Charles Black, 1970, 4th edn. (an updated version is now available); B. Ralph Lewis, *Great Civilisations: The Aztecs,* published by Ladybird Books Ltd., Loughborough, 1978. Reproduced by permission of the publishers; Staff of Stantonbury School, Milton Keynes for material from a set of worksheets entitled *Utopia;* Althea, *Bridges,* Dinosaur Publications Ltd., 1973; Macdonald Junior Reference Library, *Space,* B.P.C. publishing, 1969. Copyright © Macdonald Educational Ltd.; Hadfield, *Canals,* Basil Blackwell Publisher.

Appendix 2

1. Means and standards deviations of test scores by cohorts.
   Tables 1-3.
2. Correlations of test scores by cohorts.
   Tables 4-6.

Table 1.

Cohort A.

Means, standard deviations and standard errors of Cohort A children's scores on Ravens Matrices (Rv), NFER Reading Test (Rd1), Cohesion fiction booket (Fic), Cohesion factual booklet (Fac) and Total Cohesion materials (i.e. Fic + Fac).

Year 1. 8 year olds. N = 419

	Rv.	Rd(1)	Fic.	Fac.	C.Total
Means	30.88	21.60	18.34	10.64	28.97
s.d's	9.61	6.78	9.74	6.21	15.24
s.e's	0.47	0.33	0.48	0.30	0.75

Year 2. 9 year olds. N = 370

	Rv.	Rd(1)	Fic.	Fac.	C.Total
Means	35.80	25.51	22.39	14.71	37.10
s.d's	9.58	5.76	10.39	7.79	17.36
s.e's	0.50	0.30	0.54	0.40	0.90

Year 3. 10 year olds. N = 369

	Rv.	Rd(1)	Fic.	Fac.	C.Total
Means	39.54	27.58	25.53	17.27	42.80
s.d's	8.88	5.72	9.67	7.99	16.76
s.e's	0.47	0.30	0.50	0.42	0.88

Table 2.

Cohort B.

Means, standard deviations and standard errors of Cohort B children's scores on Ravens Matrices (Rv), NFER Reading Test (Rd1), Secondary Reading Test (Rd2) Cohesion fiction booket (Fic), Cohesion factual booklet (Fac) and Total Cohesion materials (i.e. Fic + Fac).

Year 1. 10 year olds. N = 474

	Rv.	Rd(1)	Fic.	Fac.	C.Total
Means	38.22	27.99	14.84	11.94	26.78
s.d's	8.07	5.38	7.41	6.0	12.49
s.e's	0.37	0.25	0.34	0.27	0.57

Year 2. 11 year olds. N = 322

	Rv.	Rd(2)	Fic.	Fac.	C.Total
Means	40.77	21.29	15.64	12.01	27.65
s.d's	7.27	10.78	8.17	6.54	13.41
s.e's	0.41	0.62	0.46	0.36	0.75

Year 3. 12 year olds. N = 339

	Rv.	Rd(1)	Fic.	Fac.	C.Total
Means	42.99	24.45	18.79	15.54	34.27
s.d's	6.73	11.21	8.35	7.21	14.69
s.e's	0.37	0.61	0.46	0.39	0.80

Table 3.

Cohort C.

Means, standard deviations and standard errors of Cohort B children's scores on Ravens Matrices (Rv), NFER Reading Test (Rd2), Cohesion fiction booket (Fic), Cohesion factual booklet (Fac) and Total Cohesion materials (i.e. Fic + Fac).

Year 1. 13 year olds. N = 432

	Rv.	Rd(2)	Fic.	Fac.	C.Total
Means	44.79	29.32	20.48	17.46	37.94
s.d's	6.67	11.47	7.40	6.85	13.30
s.e's	0.32	0.55	0.35	0.33	0.64

Year 2. 14 year olds. N = 386

	Rv.	Rd(2)	Fic.	Fac.	C.Total
Means	45.72	35.15	22.89	19.55	42.43
s.d's	6.63	11.04	7.72	7.81	14.56
s.e's	0.34	0.56	0.39	0.40	0.74

Year 3. 15 year olds. N = 373

	Rv.	Rd(1)	Fic.	Fac.	C.Total
Means	48.05	38.86	24.63	22.03	46.66
s.d's	6.43	11.53	7.87	8.22	15.05
s.e's	0.33	0.60	0.41	0.42	0.78

Table 4.

Cohort A.

Correlations between the children's scores on Ravens Matrices (Rv), NFER Secondary
Reading Test (Rd1). Cohesion fiction booklet (Fic). Cohesion factual booklet (Fac) and
Total Cohesion materials (i.e. Fic + Fac).
All correlation coefficients are significant. p<0.0001

Year 1. 8 year olds. N = 436

	Rv.	*Rd(1)*	*Fic.*	*Fac.*	*C.Total*
Rv.		0.510	0.522	0.531	0.550
Rd(1).			0.817	0.768	0.834
Fic.				0.820	0.972*
Fac.					0.931*
Total					

Year 2. 9 year olds. N = 380

	Rv.	*Rd(2)*	*Fic.*	*Fac.*	*C.Total*
Rv.		0.484	0.551	0.538	0.571
Rd(1).			0.768	0.730	0.787
Fic.				0.819	0.966*
Fac.					0.939*
Total					

Year 3. 10 year olds. N = 369

	Rv.	*Rd(2)*	*Fic.*	*Fac.*	*C.Total*
Rv.		0.512	0.589	0.583	0.620
Rd(1).			0.699	0.727	0.752
Fic.				0.789	0.956*
Fac.					0.935*
Total					

* These correlations here, and in Tables 5 and 6, contribute little.

Table 5.

Cohort B.

Correlations between the children's scores on Ravens Matrices (Rv), NFER Reading Test (Rd1), or Secondary Reading Test (Rd2), Cohesion fiction booklet (Fic). Cohesion factual booklet (Fac) and Total Cohesion materials (i.e. Fic + Fac).

All correlation coefficients are significant. $p < 0.0001$

Year 1. 10 year olds. N = 474

	Rv.	Rd(1)	Fic.	Fac.	C.Total
Rv.		0.516	0.505	0.494	0.535
Rd(1).			0.641	0.616	0.673
Fic.				0.745	0.948
Fac.					0.918
Total					

Year 2. 11 year olds. N = 380

	Rv.	Rd(2)	Fic.	Fac.	C.Total
Rv.		0.452	0.492	0.467	0.527
Rd(2).			0.573	0.586	0.636
Fic.				0.667	0.931
Fac.					0.894
Total					

Year 3. 12 year olds. N = 339

	Rv.	Rd(2)	Fic.	Fac.	C.Total
Rv.		0.457	0.476	0.435	0.483
Rd(1).			0.727	0.722	0.767
Fic.				0.784	0.953
Fac.					0.936
Total					

Table 6.

Cohort C.

Correlations between the children's scores on Ravens Matrices (Rv), NFER Secondary Reading Test (Rd2), Cohesion fiction booklet (Fic). Cohesion factual booklet (Fac) and Total Cohesion materials (i.e. Fic + Fac).

All correlation coefficients are significant. $p < 0.0001$

Year 1. 13 year olds. N = 432

	Rv.	*Rd(1)*	*Fic.*	*Fac.*	*C.Total*
Rv.		0.546	0.496	0.516	0.541
Rd(1).			0.665	0.704	0.732
Fic.				0.746	0.939
Fac.					0.929
Total					

Year 2. 14 year olds. N = 387

	Rv.	*Rd(2)*	*Fic.*	*Fac.*	*C.Total*
Rv.		0.495	0.457	0.488	0.483
Rd(2).			0.695	0.727	0.758
Fic.				0.757	0.937
Fac.					0.938
Total					

Year 3. 15 year olds. N = 373

	Rv.	*Rd(2)*	*Fic.*	*Fac.*	*C.Total*
Rv.		0.544	0.478	0.451	0.496
Rd(1).			0.675	0.691	0.733
Fic.				0.730	0.928
Fac.					0.932
Total					

Appendix 3

Register indexical word list
(from cohesion reading materials)

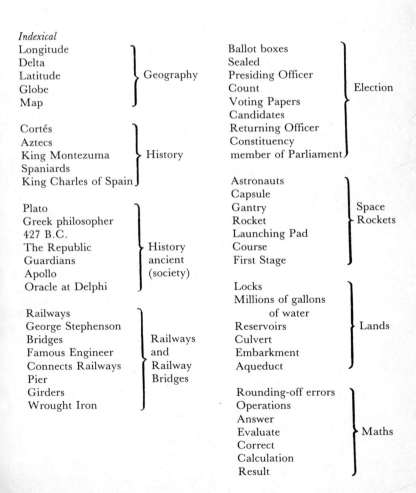

Indexical

Longitude
Delta
Latitude } Geography
Globe
Map

Cortés
Aztecs
King Montezuma } History
Spaniards
King Charles of Spain

Plato
Greek philosopher
427 B.C.
The Republic } History
Guardians   ancient
Apollo   (society)
Oracle at Delphi

Railways
George Stephenson
Bridges   Railways
Famous Engineer and
Connects Railways Railway
Pier   Bridges
Girders
Wrought Iron

Ballot boxes
Sealed
Presiding Officer
Count
Voting Papers   } Election
Candidates
Returning Officer
Constituency
member of Parliament

Astronauts
Capsule
Gantry   Space
Rocket   } Rockets
Launching Pad
Course
First Stage

Locks
Millions of gallons
        of water
Reservoirs   } Lands
Culvert
Embarkment
Aqueduct

Rounding-off errors
Operations
Answer
Evaluate   } Maths
Correct
Calculation
Result

Appendix 4

Piggy-bank (PB) example

PBs come in all sixes and shapes, though a preferred shape is that of a pig. Generally the size will range from larger than a doorknob, to smaller than a bread box. Generally money is kept in PBs, so when a child needs money he will often look for his PB. Usually, to get money out you need to be holding the bank, shake it (up and down). Generally holding it upside down makes things easier. There are less known techniques, like using a knife to help get the money out. If, when shaken, there is no sound from inside, it usually means that there is no money in the bank. If there is a sound it means that something is in there, presumably money. You shake it until the money comes out. We assume that after the money comes out it is held by the person shaking, unless we are told differently. If not enough comes out you keep shaking until you either have enough money, or no more sound is made by the shaking (i.e. the bank is empty). In general the heavier the PB the more money in it. Some piggy banks have lids which can be easily removed to get the money out. Sometimes it is necessary to smash the PB to get the money out. To put money in, you need to have the money and the bank. The money is put into the slot in the bank, at which point you are no longer directly holding the money. Money is stored in PBs for safe keeping. Often the money is kept there during the process of saving in order to buy something one wants. PBs are considered toys, and hence can be owned by children. This ownership extends to the money inside. So, for example, it is considered bad form to use money in another child's PB. Also, a PB can be played with in the same way, as, say, toy soldiers, i.e. pushed around while pretending it is alive and doing something.
After Charniak (1972)

Appendix 5

Suggested response allocations to the 4 continuum positions
(see page 78)

Responses allocated to P1
for Cohorts B and C: Item 4.10

| | | | P1 | | | | | | | | | | |
| Omissions | | Spelling | V.P.F. | | | | | | Unacceptable in 1 Cause Element (CE) | | | | |
B	C		B	C		B	C		B	C		B	C
14	9	Sid	1		War	10	5	Charles	2	1	In	1	
		Bother	1		With	3	1	Is	2		Stuart	1	
		Earns	1		Civil War	3	1	Serves	1		Who	1	
		Dom	1		Brother	2	2	Have	1		Carter	1	
		Rine	1		Son	13	4	Of	1	1	How	1	
		Forles		1	Edmund	1	1	Had	1		To		
					Parliament	1		Edward	1		So	1	
					When	1		Must	1		Together		1
					And	8	2	Oldest	1		Too		1
								Queens	1		There		1
								Was					
			5	1		41	17		13	2		7	3

Cohort B	14	5	41	13	7	B = 80 17.8%
Cohort C	9	1	17	2	3	C = 32 7.2%

Responses allocated to P2
for Cohorts B and C : Item 4.10: Forces

Satisfying 1 CE only + kingship

	B	C
Cohorts		
Throne	3	1
Coronation	1	
Castle	1	
Crown	1	
1 Ring	6	7
Royalty	1	
2 Place (?)	2	
3 Rule	1	1
Horses	1	
Name	1	
Attention	1	
5 Miniature	1	
6 Hand	1	
Letter ?	1	
Cohort B	**18**	
Cohort C		**5**

P2 — Satisfying 1 or more CE's + kingship

	B	C
Family	9	5
Father	1	
Daughter	1	
Wife	1	
7 Brothers	1	
Sister	1	
Home		1
8 Man	1	
Slave	1	
Servant	1	1
9 Festival ?	1	
10 Friend	2	
Feast	1	
Cohort B	**21**	
Cohort C		**7**

Satisfying 2 or more CE's + kingship

	B	C
Kingdom	1	
Palace	10	1
Court	1	
Council	1	
Region (?)	1	
House	3	
Nation		1
Table		1
Cohort B	**17**	
Cohort C		**3**

Satisfying 2 or more CE's + Join

	B	C
Side	10	9
Club	1	1
Gang	1	
Men	2	6
Party	1	1
Police		1
Union		1
	16	**16**

B = 72	**C = 31**

Notes

CE = Clause Element

1. Ring is prominent in passage
2. Place = Palace ?
3. All the King's Horses?
4. As in 'Open in the Name of the King'?
5. Prominent in passage
6. Associated with 1 and 5
7. Could be V.P.F
8. In the sense of 'The King's Man'
9. Doubtful
10. The King's Friend?

Responses allocated to P3 and 4 for Cohorts B and C: Item 4.10

	P3						**P4**	
	Satisfying						Author's Word	
	2 or more CE's + Military Chain						Replaced	
Cohorts	B	C		B	C		B	C
Battle	5	3	Navy	3		Forces	5	14
Armoury	1		Army	286	321	Force	1	1
Legion	1	1	Soldiers	4	4			
Defence(s)		3	Regiment	3	10			
Defense		1	Troop(s)	5	9			
Loyalists		1	Knights	2	1			
Followers		1	Warriors	1				
Guard(s)	2	8	Services	1				
Own	1		Cavalry		3			
Fight	1		Ranks		1			
Cohort B	11			305	B = 31·6		6	B = 6
Cohort C		18		349	C = 367		15	C = 15

Appendix 6

Different types of genre styles

Special Kinds of Writing

(a) John was not the only boy involved but it seems to me that since his was the leading role in this unfortunate incident I must...

(b) It came slowly towards the crowd, its eyes glaring, its teeth bared. The people in the crowd stood stock-still, frozen with fear while...

(c) And so it came to pass that on the fourth day the men, women and children came out from the city into the valley below and...

(d) Just can't help myself – It's you, it's you – You're the one ooh I need...

(e) I am 16 years of age and just about to leave shcool after taking my CSE examinations. I am interested...

(f) To release the cylinder block, first slacken off the camshaft chain tensioner. Then unscrew and remove the single bolt at the rear...

(g) Lovely Eleanor, 18, is training to be an air hostess and tells us that she can't wait to fly...

(h) Didn't do much today. A. came around in the afternoon and we just sat around and talked...

(i) Pinchas Zukerman began his mastery of the violin when he was eight. Two years later he won a scholarship...

(j) Now when the little Dwarf heard that he was to dance a second time before the Queen he was so proud that...

(k) With their album already flying high, the band are planning a number of gigs...

(l) I know how difficult it must be for you – but be patient because in just a few weeks time we'll be together...

(m) Stir in the sugar, with a swift motion and simmer over a very low heat, adding more milk if necessary...

(n) After last month's fun and games you're due for a slow down. Watch out for some odd events next week...

(o) And what's more your cat will simply love the juicy flavour of...

(p) In case of emergency press the red button and wait until the machine stops. Do not...

(q) Your postal order is enclosed herewith. We regret any inconvenience caused by our inability to send the goods you require...

From Raleigh, M. (1981) 'Special Kinds of Writing', *The Language Book*. London, ILEA English Centre.

References

Albsu (1987), *Adult Literacy*. London. Adult Literacy and Basic Skills Unit.

Anderson, E. (1983), Cohesion and the teacher. Australian Journal of Reading. Vol. 6. No.1. 35-42.

Anderson, J. (1976), Psycholinguistic Experiments in Foreign Language Testing. St Lucia. Queensland. University of Queensland Press.

Anderson, J. (1981), GAP analysis in the perception of textual cohesion. Faculty of Educational Studies. The Open University.

Anderson, J. (1983), The writer, the reader and the text. In Gillham, B. (ed.), *Reading Through the Curriculum*. London. Heinemann. 82-94.

Anderson, J. (1984), The computer as tutor, tutee, tool in reading and language. Reading Vol. 18. No. 2. 67-78.

Anderson, J. (1987), Micro Tales. Reading. Vol. 21. No. 1. 4-15.

Anderson, R.C. and P.D. Pearson (1984), A Schema – Theoretic View of Basic Processes in Reading. In Pearson *et al.* (1984).

Anderson, R.C., E.H. Heibert, J.A. Scott and I.A. Wilkinson (1985), *Becoming a Nation of Readers: the Report of the Commission on Readers*. Urbana Champagne. Illinois. The Center for the Study of Reading.

Baker, L. and A.L. Brown, Metacognitive Skills in Reading. In Pearson *et al.* (1984).

Bartlett, F.C. (1932), *Remembering*. Cambridge. Cambridge University Press.

Benson, J and W. Greaves (1973), *The Language People Really Use*. Agincourt Ontario. Book Society of Canada.

Berdiansky, B., B. Gunwell and J. Kohler (1969), Spelling-sound relationships and primary form-class descriptions for speech comprehension vocabularies of six to nine year olds. Southwest Regional Laboratory for Educational Research and Development. Technical Report No. 15. Cited in Smith F. (1971) *Understanding Reading*. New York. Holt, Rinehart & Winston.

Berry, M. (1977), *Introduction to Systemic Linguistics 1. Structures and Systems*. London. Batsford.

Binkley, M.R. (1983), A Descriptive and Comparative Study of Cohesion Structure in Test Materials from Differing Academic Disciplines. Unpublished PhD Dissertation. The George Washington University.

Binkley, M.R. (1986), *Becoming a Nation of Readers: Implications for Teachers*. Washington. OERI.

Bloom D. and J. Green (1984), In Pearson *al.* (1984).

Bridge C.A. and P.N. Winograde (1982), Reader's awareness of cohesive relationships during cloze comprehension. Journal of Reading Behaviour. Vol. XIV. No.3. 299-312.

Bronfenbrenner U. (1976), The experimental ecology of education. Teachers College Record, 78. 157-204.

Chapman, L.J. (1970), The Acquisition of Language Skills by Children. Unpublished MSc thesis, University of Aston in Birmingham.

Chapman, L.J. (1979a), The perception of language cohesion during fluent reading. In Kolers, P.A., M.E. Wrolstad and H. Bouma (eds), *Processing of Visible Language*). Vol. 1. New York. Plenum.

Chapman, L.J. (1979b), Pedagogical strategies for fluent reading, In Thackray D. (ed.), *Growth in reading*. London. Ward lock, 147-154.

Chapman, L.J. (1979c), Confirming children's use of cohesion ties. The Reading teacher. Vol. 33. No. 3. 317-322.

Chapman, L.J. (1980), The Reader and the Text. Presidential Address. In Chapman L.J. (1981) (ed.), *The Reader and the Text*. London. Heinemann. 1-15.

Chapman, L.J. (1981), The development of the perception of textual cohesion. Paper presented at the 25th Annual I.R.A. convention St Louis U.S.A. ERIC ED. 192-260.

Chapman, L.C. (1983a), *Reading Development and Cohesion*. London. Heinemann Educational Books.

Chapman, L.J. (1983b), A Study in Reading Development: a comparison of the ability of 8-, 10-, and 13-year-old children to perceive cohesion in their school texts. In Gillham, B. (ed.), *Reading Through the Curriculum*. London. Heinemann. 165-178.

Chapman, L.J. (1985), A reading Development Continuum: A Framework for the Teaching of Reading? In Burnes, D., H. French and F. Moore (eds.), *Literacy: Strategies and Perspectives*. Adeline S. Austrailia. Austrailian Reading Association. 155-165.

Chapman, L.J. and E. Anderson (1982), Children's perception of texual cohesion. In K. Tuunainen and A. Chiaroni (eds), *Full Participation*. Joensu. Finland. The University of Joensu. 139-156.

Chapman, L.J. and A. Stokes (1980), Developmental trends in the perception of textural cohesion. In Kolers, P.A., M.E. Wrolstad and H. Bouma (eds), *Processing of Visible Language*. Vol. 2. New York. Plenum.

Charniak E. (1968), Towards a model of children's story comprehension. Unpublished Ph.D. thesis. Massuchusetts Institute of Technology.

Cromsky, N. (1957), *Syntactic Structures*. The Hague. Mouton.

Cromsky, N. (1965), *Aspects of a Theory of Syntax*. Cambridge (Mass), The M.I.T. Press.

Clay, M.M. (1972), *The Early Detection of REading Difficulties: a diagnostic survey*. Auckland N.Z. Heinemann.

Clay, M.M. (1972), *The Early Detection of Reading Difficulties: a diagnostic survey*. Auckland H.Z. Heinemann.

Cook-Gumperz, J. (1986), Literacy and schooling: An unchanging education? In Cook-Gumperz (ed.), *The Social Construction of Literacy*. New York. Cambridge University Press. 2-44.

Donaldson, M. (1978), *Children's Minds*. Glasgow. Fontana/Collins.

Downing, J. (1970), Children's concepts of language in learning to read. Educational Research. Vol. 12. 106-112.

Downing, J. (1976), The reading instruction register. Language Arts. Vol. 53. 762-766. 780.

Esau H. (1982), The 'smoking-gun' tape: Analysis of the information structure in the Nixon tapes. Text Vol. 2. No. 4. 293-322.

Flavell, J.H. (1978) Metacognitive development. In Scandura, J.M. and C.J. Braienerd (eds), *Structural/process theories of complex human behaviour*. Alphen a.d. Rijn, The Netherlands: Sijthoff and Noordhoff.

Freebody, P. and R.C. Anderson (1983), Effects of vocabulary difficulty, text cohesion and schema availability on reading comprehension. Reading Reasearch Quarterly. Vol. 18. No. 3 277-294.

Garber M.D. (1979), An examination and comparison of selected cohesive features found in child-produced texts and beginning reading materials. Unpublished Ph.D. dissertation. Georgia State University. Georgia. U.S.A.

Gee, J.P. (1986), Orality and Literacy: From the Savage Mind to Ways with Words. Review Article in TESOL Quarterly 20,4, pp 716-746.

Glaser (1985), In Anderson *et al.* (1985).

Gollasch, F.V. (1982), *Language and Literacy. The Selected Writings of Kenneth S. Goodman*. Vol. 1. Process, Theory, Research. London. Routledge & Kegan Paul.

Goodman, K.S. (1970), The Reading Process; Theory and Practice. In Gollasch, F.V. (1982).

Goodman, K.S. (1973), Miscues: Windows on the Reading Process. In Gollasch, F.V. (1982) 93-102.

Goodman, K.S. (1975), Influences of the visual peripheral fields in reading. Research in the Teaching of English. Vol. 9. No. 2. 210-222.

Gorman, T. (1986) *The Framework for the Assessment of Language*. Windsor. NFER/Nelson.

Gough, P.B. (1985) One second of reading: postcript. In Singer H. and R.B. Ruddell (eds), (3rd Edition), *Theoretical Models and Processes in Reading*. Newark Del. International Reading Association.

Graham, K.E. and H.A. Robinson (1984), *Study Skills Handbook*. Newark, N.J. International Reading Association.

Graves, D.H. (1983), *Writing: teachers and Children at Work*. Melbourne. Heinemann.

Gregory, M. and S. Carroll (1978), *Language and Situation: Language Varieties and their Social Contexts*. London. Routledge and Kegan Paul.

Gutwinski W. (1976), *Cohesion in Literacy Texts*. The Hague. Mouton.

Hadley, I.L. (1985), Perception of Anaphoric Personal Reference Items in Continuous Text, by Primary School Readers at Three Year Levels. Unpublished M.Ed. Dissertation. The Flinders University of South Australia.

Halliday, M.A.K. (1975), *Learning How to Mean*. London. Arnold.

Halliday, M.A.K. (1978), *Language as Social Semiotic*. London. Arnold.

Halliday, M.A.K. (1985), *Introduction to Functional Grammer*. London. Arnold.

Halliday, M.A.K. and R. Hasan (1976), *Cohesion in English*. London. Longman.

Halliday, M.A.K. and R. Hasan (1980), *Text and Context*. Sophia Linguistica VI. Tokyo. Sophia University.

Harrison (1979), Assessing the readability of school texts. In Lunzer, E.A. and Gardner K. (1979).

Hasan, R. (1984), Coherance and cohesive harmony. In Flood, J. (ed.), *Understanding Reading Comprehension*. Newark. N.J. International Reading Association.

Heath, S.B. (1983), *Ways with Words*. Cambridge. Cambridge University Press.

Hirsch, E.D. Jr (1987), *Cultural Literacy*. Boston. Houghton Mifflin.

Hoey M.P. (1983), *On the Surface of Discourse*. London. Allen and Unwin.

Hoffman, M. (1977), *Reading, Writing and Relevance*. Sevenoaks. Hodder and Stoughton/UKRA.

Huey, E.B. (1908), *The Psychology and Pedagogy of Reading*. MacMillan Co. Paperback Edition (1968). Cambridge Mass M.I.T. Press.

Irwin, J.W. (1980), The effects of linguistic cohesion on prose comprehension. Journal of Reading Behaviour. Vol. 12. 325-332.

Just, M.A. and P.A. Carpenter (1977), *Cognitive Processes in Comprehension*. Hillside NJ. L.E.A.

Kavanagh, J.F. and I.G. Mattingly (eds) (1972), *Language by Ear and by Eye. The Relationships between Speech and Reading*. Cambridge. Mass. The M.I.T. Press.

Keys, W. (1987), *Aspects of Science Education in English Schools*. London. NFER-Nelson.

Kintsch, W. (1977), *Memory and Cognition*. New York. Wiley.

Kress, G.R. (1982), *Learning to Write*. London. Routledge & Kegan Paul.

Laberge D. and S.J. Samuels (1977), *Basic Processes in Reading*. Hillsdale N.J. L.E.A. Press.

Langer J. (1981), In Chapman L.J. (ed.), *The Reader and the Text*. London Heinemann 125-130.

Lunzer, E.A. and Gardner, K. (1979), *The Effective Use of Reading*. London. Heinemann Eduational Books.

Mackay D., B. Thompson and P. Schaub (1968), *Breakthrough to Literacy Manual*. London. Longman for the Schools Council.

Marzano, R.J. (1984), A cluster approach to vocabulary instruction: A new direction from the research literature. The Reading Teacher Vol. 38. No. 2. 168-172.

McCulley G.A. (1983), Writing quality, coherence and cohesion. D. of Ed. Dissertation, Utah State Unviersity, Utah U.S.A.

Meyer, B.J.F. and G.E. Rice, The Structure of Text. In Pearson *et al.* (1984).

Miller. G.A. (1972), Reflections on the Conference. In Kavenagh J.F. and I.E. Mattingly (eds) pp. 373-381.

Moberly P.C. (1978), Elementary Children's Understanding of Anaphoric Relationships in Connected Discourse. Unpublished Doctoral Dissertation. Northwestern University, Illinois.

Monson D. (n.d), Effect of type and direction on comprehension of anaphoric relationships. Unpublished research paper. University of Washington.

Morgan, R. (1986). *Helping Children Read*. London. Methuen.

Morgan J.L. and M.B. Sellner (1980), Discourse and Linguistic Theory. In Spiro R.J., B.C. Bruce and W.F. Brewer (eds), *Theoretical Issues in Reading Comprehension*. Hillsdale N.J. L.E.A.

Morris, J.M. (1984), Focus on Phonics: Phonics 44 for initial literacy in English. Reading Vol. 18. No. 1. 13-24.

Mosenthal, J.H. and R.J. Tierney (1981), The cohesion concept's relationship to the coherence of text. Technical Report No. 22. Center for the Study of Reading, University of Illinois, Urbana, Champaign.

Nunan D. (1983a), Discourse Processing by First Language, second Phase and Second Language Learners. Unpublished Ph.D. Thesis. The Flinders University of South Austrailia.

Nunan D. (1983b), Distance as a factor in the resolution of cohesive ties in secondary texts. Austrailian Journal of Reading. Vol. 6. No. 1. 30-34.

Pearson, P.D., R. Barr, M.L. Kamil and P. Mosenthal (eds) (1984), *Handbook of Reading Research.* New York. Longman.

Perera, K. (1987), Understanding Language. In Mercer N. (ed.), *Language and Literacy from an Educational Perspective.* Vol. 2. In School. Milton Keynes. Open University Press.

Pettegrew B.S. (1981), Text formation: A comparative study of literate and pre-literate first grade children. Unpublished Ph.D. dissertation. The Ohio State University. U.S.A.

Philips J.M. and S. Zinan (1980), Cohesion and readability: cohesive ties in basal reading series, grades 1-6. In Chapman L.J. (ed.) (1981), *The Reader and the Text.* London. Heinemann.

Pumfrey, P.D. (1986), Paired reading: promise and pitfalls. Educational Research Vol. 28. No. 2. 89-94.

Reid, J.F. (1984) Into print: reading and language growth. In Barnes, P., J. Oates, L.J. Chapman, V. Lee, and P. Czerniewska (eds), *Personality, Development and Learning.* Sevenoaks. Hodder and Stoughton/OU.

Rhodes, L.K. (1979), The Interaction of Beginning Readers' Strategies and Texts Reflecting Alterate Models of Predictability. Unpublished PhD. Dissertation. Indiana University, Bloomington, USA.

Rumelhart, D.E. (1975) Notes on a schema for stories. In Bobrow, D.G. and A.M. Collins (eds), *Representation and Understanding.* New York. Academic Press.

Rumelhart, D.E. (1977), Toward an interactive model of reading. In Dornic, S. (ed.), *Attention and Performance.* V1. Hillsdale, N.J.Erlbaum.

Rumelhart, D.E. (1980), Schemata: the building blocks of cognition. In Spiro, R.J., B.C., Bruce and W.F. Brewer, (eds), *Theoretical Issues in Reading Comprehension.* Hillsdale, N.J. Erlbaum.

Rutter, P. and B. Raban, (1982), The development of cohesion in childrens' writing: a preliminary investigation. First Language. Vol. 3. 63-75.

Smith, F. (1978), *Reading.* Cambridge. Cambridge University Press.

Smith J. (1985), Semantic Aspects of Cohesion. Unpublished Ph.D. dissertation. University of Queensland.

Smith J. and J. Elkins (1984), Comprehending cohesion. Reading Vol. 18. No.3 153-159.

Smith J. and J. Elkins (1985), The use of cohesion by underachieving readers. Reading Psychology Vol. 6. Nos. 1-2. 13-25.

Southgate, V., H. Arnold and S. Johnson (1981), *Extending Beginning Reading.* London. Heinemann Educational Books.

Stedman, L.C. and C.F. Kaestle (1987), Literacy and reading performance in the United States, from 1880 to the present. Reading Research Qarterly. Vol. XX11 No. 1. 8-46.

Stewart-Dore, N. (ed.) (1986), *Writing and Reading to Learn* Rozelle NSW. Australia. Primary English Teaching Association.

Street, B.V. (1984), *Literacy in Theory and Practice.* Cambridge University Press.

Tann S. (1987), Topic Work: a mismatch of perceptions. Reading Vol. 21. No. 1. 62-70.

Tizard, J., W. N. Scholfield and J. Hewison (1982), Collaboration between teachers and parents in assisting children's reading. British Journal of Educational Psychology. Vol. 52. No. 1. 1-15.

Topping, K. (1986), W.H.I.C.H. Parental involvement in reading scheme? A guide for practioners. Reading Vol. 20. No. 3. 148-156.

Tuinman J.J. (1973/1974), Determining the passage dependency of comprehension questions in five major tests. Reading Research Quarterly Vol. 9. 206-223. ·

Vygotsky, L.S. (1962), *Thought and Language.* Cambridge (Mass.). The M.I.T. Press.

Waterland, L. (1985), *Read With Me. An Apprenticeship Approach to Reading.* Stroud, Glos. The Thimble Press.

Weir, R.H. (1962), *Language in the Crib.* The Hague. Mouton.

Whimbey, A. (1975), *Intelligence Can Be Taught.* New York. Dutton.

Williams R. (1983), Teaching the recognition of cohesive ties in reading a foreign language. Reading in a Foreign Language. Vol. 1. No. 1 35-52.

Wishart E. (1987) Textual cohesion and effective reading. Reading Vol 21. No. 1. 30-42.

Worrall A. (1985), Patterns of comprehension in third grade. Australian Journal of Reading. Vol. 8. No. 1. 45–48.

Yde P. and M. Spoelders (1985), Text cohesion: An exploratory study with beginning writers. Applied Linguistics. 6. 407–416.

Index

additive conjunction ties   25, 27
adult literacy   ix–x
adversative conjunction ties   25, 27
analysis technique   74–82
anaphora   92
anaphoric cohesion
    definition   41
    research   43, 44, 45
anchor passage   65–7
assessing needs, of
    P1 children   101
    P2 children   105
    P3 children   108
    P4 children   111
    junior children   117
assessment of reading   94
    P1 children   104
    P2 children   107
    P3 children   110
    P4 children   114
    junior children   126–7
Assessment of Performance Unit   31, 57, 94, 95
authors, discussions of   109–110, 113–4
autonymy   27

bottom-up model   5–6, 90

cataphoric cohesion   41, 43

causal conjunction ties   25, 27
chaining   26–7
    and cohesive ties   91–2
    and metacognition   92–3
clausal ellipsis ties   25
clausal substitution ties   25
clines   18, 28–9
cloze procedure   58, 60
    definition   41
    research into   44–5
clusters   120–1
co-classification   46
code, and reading   3–5, 7
co-extension   25, 26–7, 46
cohesion   21, 28, 43, 57, 91
    analysis   42, 46
    and reading development   93–4
    definition   22
    research   41–51, 128
        and reading   41–7
        and writing   47–9
        criticisms of   49–51, 129–30
cohesive chains   91–3, 96
cohesive ties
    defined   22
    examples of   23–5
    in research   27
    in writing   47–9
    testing of   58–9
collocation   23, 27, 47
comparative ties   24

comprehension
  research into   52–3
  problems of testing   57
  and cohesion testing   63–4
computers   13–14
  and literacy   x
  for infants   106–7, 109, 113
  for juniors   124–6
conjoining   25, 26
conjunction group of cohesive
    ties   23, 25, 48, 58
conjunctive relationships   47
continuum of reading   75
consensus measurements   65–6
co-reference   25, 26, 46
curriculum material, for
    assessment   94, 95
curriculum needs, and receding
    93

deletion procedure   111
demonstrative ties   24
dialects   9–10
directed reading activities   121
discussions, with juniors   119–20

ecological validity   56
ellipsis group of cohesive ties   23,
    24–5, 48
emergent literacy   11–12, 98–9
employers, and literacy   ix–x
ethnic minority groups   47
evaluation of teaching
  P1 children   104
  P2 children   107
  P3 children   110
  P4 children   114
  junior children   126
exophoric   41
explicit cohesion   63

family background and reading
    98–9

field of discourse   28–9, 93
function
  of childrens' language   19–20
  of adults' language   20–22

GAP analysis   58, 59, 64, 65–6,
    77
genre   27–8, 29, 93, 119
grammar   9–10, 18
group cloze   121–2
group prediction   122
group sequencing   122
group SQ3R   122

Halliday, M.A.K.   17–29, 37,
    49–51, 90, 128, 129, 130
Headstart project   10
home influence   10–12
home-school relationship   13
hyponymy   27

ideational function   20
Incas, communication system   13
individual profiles   83–8
infant school, teaching of
    reading   98–114
information
  age of   x, 13–14
  and power   14
  theory   65
  structure   21
instructional research   40–1
interactive model of reading   7,
    90
interpersonal function   20
inter sentential cohesion   61, 62
intra sentential cohesion   61

junior school, teaching of reading
    115–27

language
  and thought   102
  development   7-8
Language Development Course,
  OU.   54
lexical group of cohesive ties   23,
  47, 48, 58
lexicogrammatical system   18-19
linguistic awareness   8-9
linguistics, and reading   7

Manchester University research
  project   53-4, 118, 130
meaning   7, 18, 20, 21-2
meronomy   27
metacognition   36, 90-3
microcomputers   106-7, 109, 113
miscue analysis   39, 57, 45, 46
mind, and reading   2-3
mode   28-9, 93
models of reading
  bottom-up   5-6, 90
  interactive   7, 90
  top-down   6-7, 90
monofunctional   19
multi-lingual problems   9, 11

National Assessment of
  Educational Progress   48
nominal ellipsis ties   24
nominal substitution ties   24
non cohesive elements   60-1
non-fiction reading   108, 109,
  112, 119
Nottingham University research
  project   52-3, 74, 94, 118,
  121, 130

Open University research project
  aims   55-6
  philosophy   56-9

results   66-74, 82-8
summary of findings   88-9

paired reading   13, 103
Perception of Cohesion
  project   92
permanence, of writing   33
personal ties   24
phonemes/graphemes   18
position 1 (P1) readers   100-4
position 2 (P2) readers   104-7
position 3 (P3) readers   108-111
position 4 (P4) readers   112
pre-reading plan (PReP)   120,
  123
presupposition   25-6, 91-2
prior knowledge, and tests   63-4
process, reading as   16
product, reading as   16
profile system, of assessment
  96-7
'proposition' in text structure
  36-7
psychology, and reading   1-2,
  32-8, 90-1

rank scale   18-19
readability formulae   41-2
reading development   90, 93-7
Reading Development Continuum
  (RDC)   75-78, 100-114,
  117-127
  individual profiles   83-9
  plotting responses   78-9
  position 1 children   79-80,
    100-4
  position 2 children   80-1, 104-7
  position 3 children   81, 107-110
  position 4 children   82, 110-114
  junior children   82-3, 117-8
'reading readiness'   11-12
reading process   3-5, 22

reading, to and with children
  position 1   103
  position 2   105–6
  position 3   119
  position 4   112
  juniors   119
recategorization, on RDC   76–7
redundancy   4
reference group of cohesive ties
    23, 24, 48, 58
referential relationships   47
reflection, on reading   52–3, 91,
    93–4, 95
register   22, 28
  testing of   57, 62
reiteration ties   23, 47
Report on the Commission on
    Reading USA   31–2, 105
research, into reading
  at Manchester University   53–4
  at Nottingham University
    52–3, 129
  at the Open University   54–89,
    129
  in USA   31–2, 33, 34, 40, 48,
    105, 129

schema   33–4
  development   102
  research   33–5
  theory   90–1
school-parent relationships   99,
    115–6
second language pupils   11
semantics   18
semantic interpretation rules   38
silent reading   112
socio-economic level, and
    achievement   116
socialization, and reading   39–40
social perspective on language   17
sociolinguistic perspective, on
    research   39
sounds/writing   18
Standard English   9–10

standards, of home and school
    10–11
study skills   122–4
substitution, group of cohesive
    ties   23, 24, 44, 48
synonymy   27
syntax   18, 38
systemic linguistics   17, 18, 28

teaching programme
  for infants   99–114
  for juniors   116–127
temporal conjunction ties   25, 27
tenor   28–9, 93
text processing   90–1
text structure   36, 91
texture   21, 22, 28, 47, 48, 91,
    93–4
theme/rheme   21
thinking
  and language   90–1, 102
  and reading   2–3
tie distance   42
top-down model   6–7

UKRA conference   44

values, of home and school
    10–11
verbal ellipsis ties   24
verbal substitution ties   24
vocabulary, and juniors   120

wholistic approach   12, 129
writing, for reading for
  P1 children   103–4
  P2 children   106
  P3 children   109
  P4 children   112–3
  juniors   124

'zone of proximal development'
    102